Carving Caricature Busts

W. "Pete" LeClair

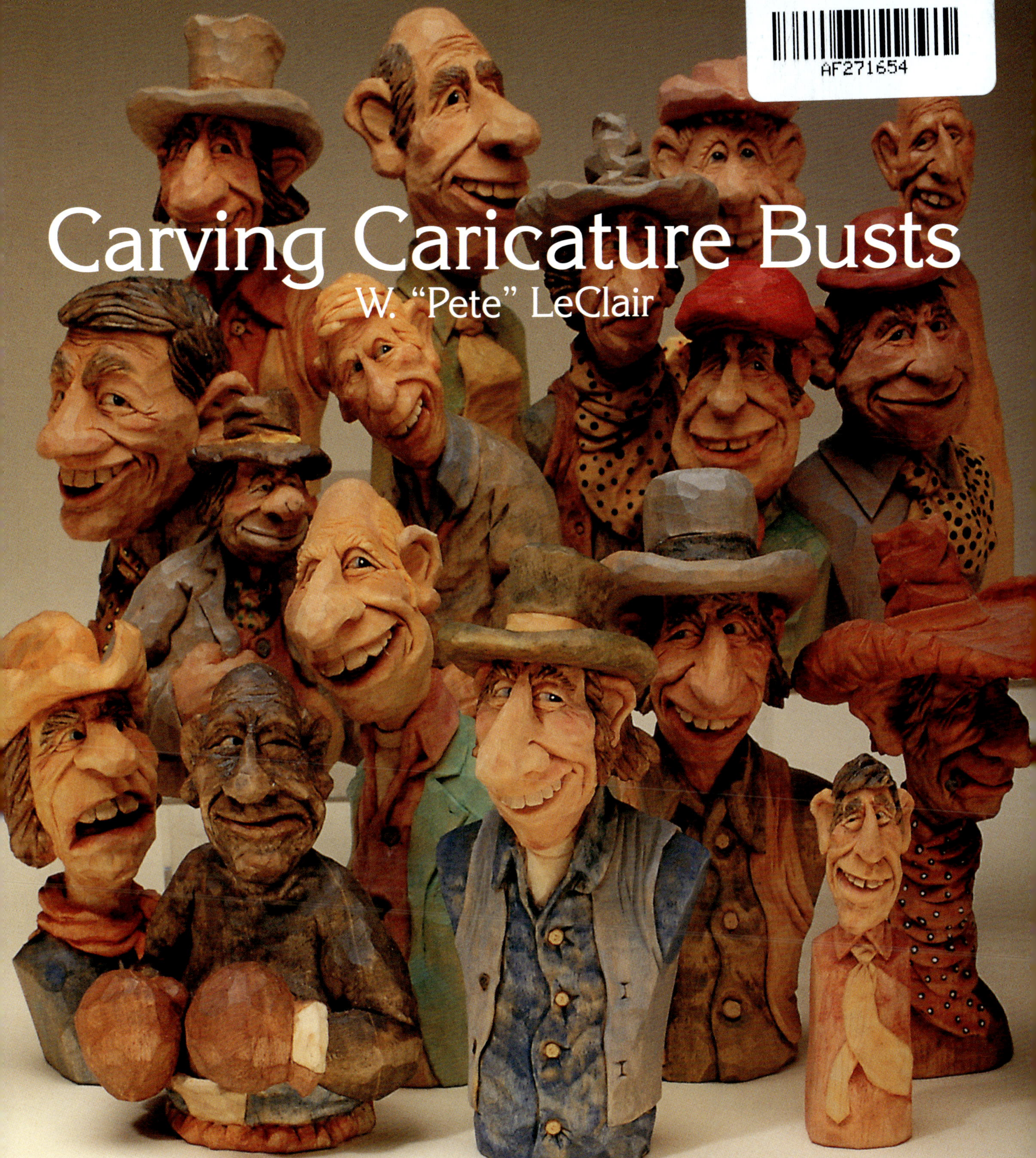

Schiffer Publishing Ltd

4880 Lower Valley Road • Atglen, PA 19310

Contents

Copyright © 2002 by Pete LeClair
Library of Congress Card Number: 2001099721

Designed by John P. Cheek
Cover design by Bruce M. Waters
Type set in Korinna BT/Korinna BT

ISBN: 978-0-7643-1497-1
Printed in China
5 4 3 2

Published by Schiffer Publishing Ltd.
4880 Lower Valley Road
Atglen, PA 19310
Phone: (610) 593-1777; Fax: (610) 593-2002
E-mail: Schifferbk@aol.com
Please visit our web site catalog at
www.schifferbooks.com

We are always looking for people to write books on new and related subjects. If you have an idea for a book please contact us at the above address.

This book may be purchased from the publisher.
Please try your bookstore first.
You may write for a free catalog.

Introduction

When my publisher asked me to consider doing a third book, it took me quite a while to figure out what to do. People have said very kind things about the first two books, and I appreciate that very much. But I wasn't sure what I could add to what I had already said.

Finally it occurred to me that what people seem to like about what I do is the detail work of the carving. So why not give them more details? This new book uses the bust as a way to go more deeply into the things I try to do to make a caricature carving come alive. The bust is nice because it doesn't require the attention to the rest of the body, focusing just on the torso and the head. With over 350 photographs in this book, this means that each step is broken down into its separate elements, which, I hope, will make it very clear to the reader how to do it.

In the back of the book is a gallery of 25 other busts I have carved. Some are similar to the one carved in the book, and some are quite different. There are also patterns for several of the carvings, though many were created without a pattern, starting from scratch.

In the photos you will notice that my holding hand is covered with a carving glove, and that the thumb of my knife hand has a very heavy coating of tape on it. As I mentioned in my last book, a few years ago one of the little nicks that carvers always seem to get, became very infected, spreading beyond the finger, and becoming life-threatening. As a safety precaution I simply tape several layers of masking tape over my thumb, keeping the blade from getting to the skin. In this time of growing concern of super germs, it seems wise to use a little simple precaution.

I hope you enjoy the book and that you carve safely.

Carving Tools

I often get questions about the tools I use, so for this book I have included a photograph of the various knives and gouges. It is not very fancy or very large, but it serves me well.

These are the tools I use in this project.

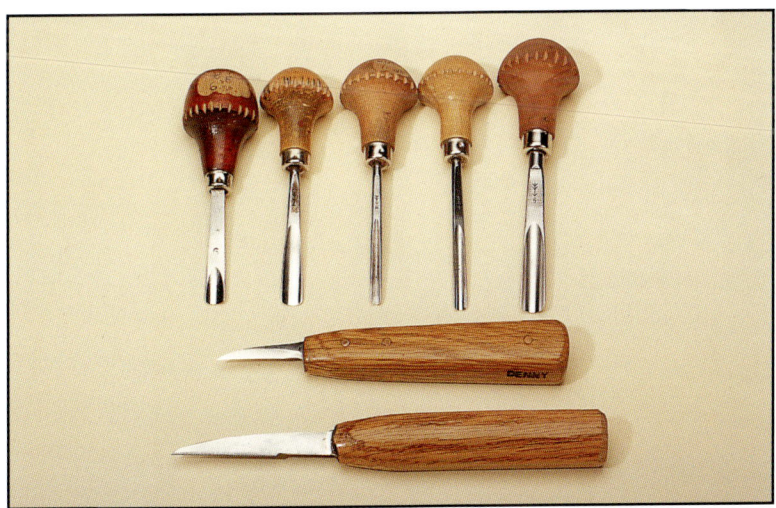

Across the top are the gouges (left to right) Harmen #9, 3/8"; Swiss #7/8mm; Swiss #11/3mm; Swiss #9/5mm; Swiss #9/10mm.
At the bottom are the two knives. The top is a Denny knife, with a 1-7/8" straight blade, used for detailing. Below it is a heavy duty knife, with a 3-1/2" blade, used for blocking out.

The Carving Project

Main pattern, 6" tall

The block is bass wood, 6" x 3" x 3".

Use the pattern to draw the side profile…

and the front view on two adjacent sides

The result.

Cut the front view first on the bandsaw, leaving the cuts incomplete. This holds the piece together for the profile cut.

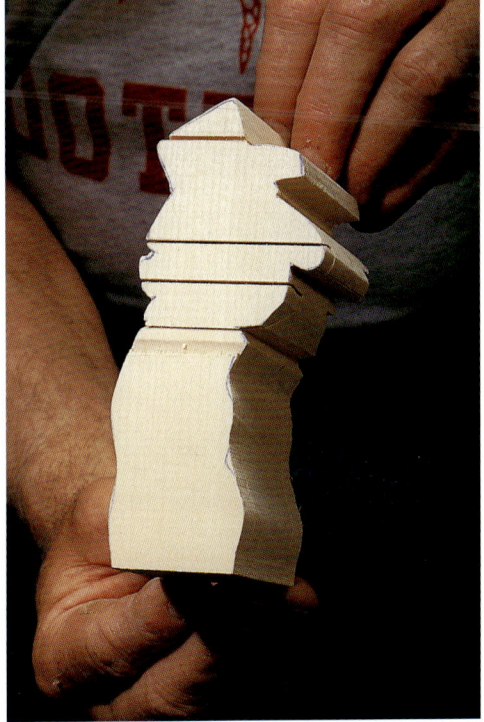

Cut the profile out completely.

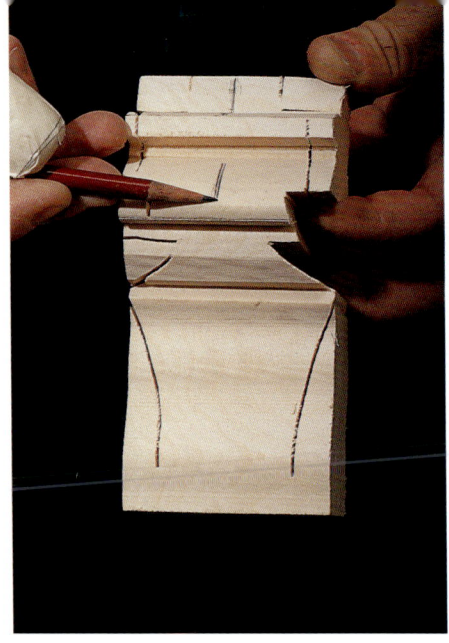

Draw a center line all the way around the blank. It is easier to do this while the blank still has the side edges intact.

The result. At the bottom of the side you can see where the excess was broken off.

With the bandsaw doing most of the work, all you need to do to remove the excess wood is stick the knife in…

Draw in the top of the hat brim…

and give it a twist. The piece should break right off. Continue this around the blank.

and the bottom.

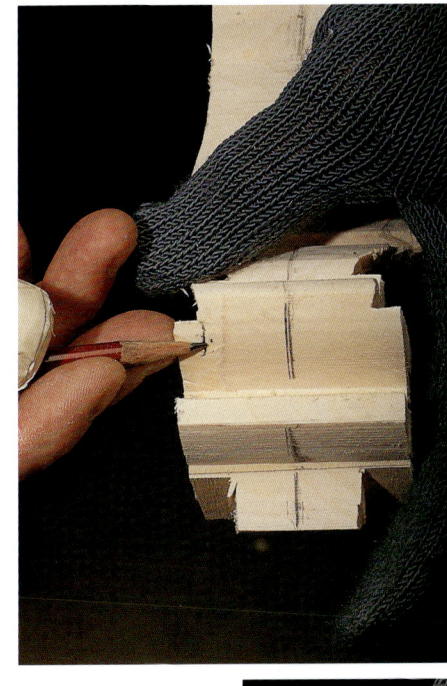

Determine the widest point of the head, which will be either the ears or the hair over the ears. You can make the head fatter or thinner by adjusting this line.

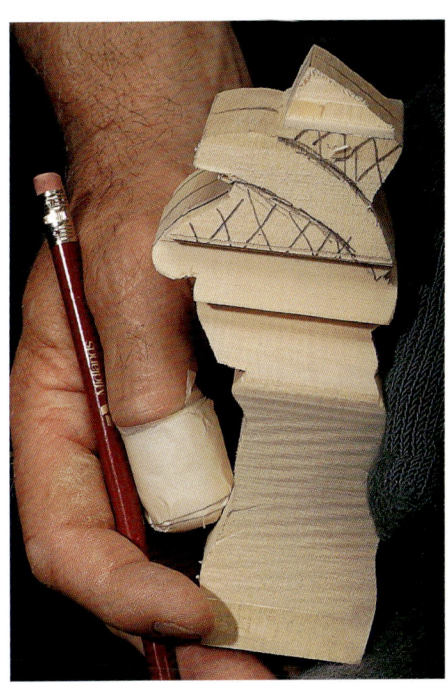

The shaded area will be cut out.

Repeat on the other side of the face.

I remove this area around the crown by cutting in lightly (I'm going with the grain), and slicing it away.

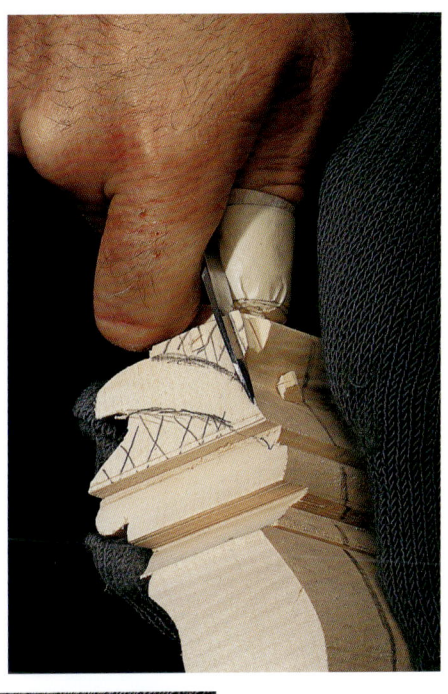

I often mark the area to be removed with pencil lines.

The result.

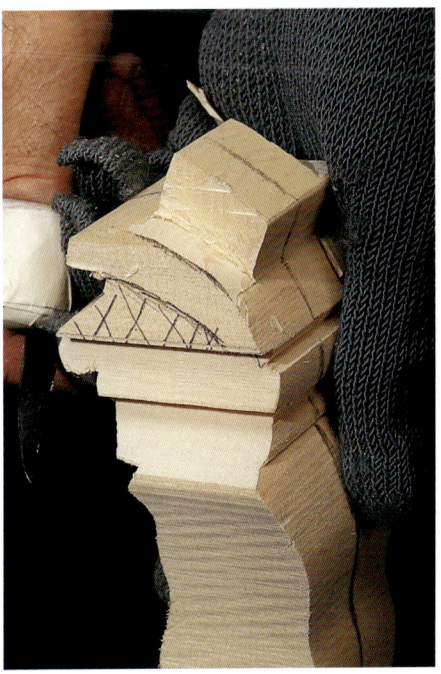

Under the brim I use a Swiss #9/10mm gouge. Start at the back and gouge about half way. This is for safety reasons. I always work toward the center.

Come back along the side of the face to clean up the cut. Repeat on the other side.

Come back from the other side.

Progress

The bandsaw leaves a little excess here at the collar line.

A flatter gouge cleans up the areas the #9 did not reach. Cut in under the brim, cup side of the gouge down.

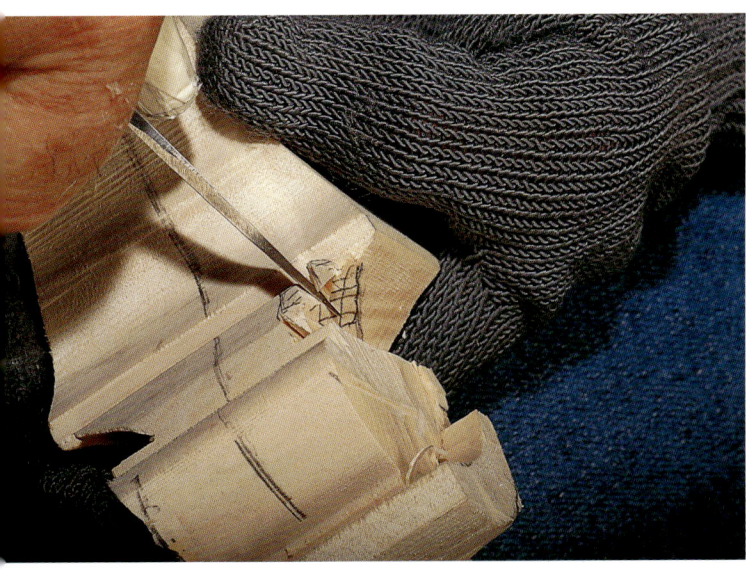

To remove it make a stop cut with the grain…

Find the approximate center of the side of the head and draw a line. This is almost the center of the ears.

and come back to it from the shoulder.

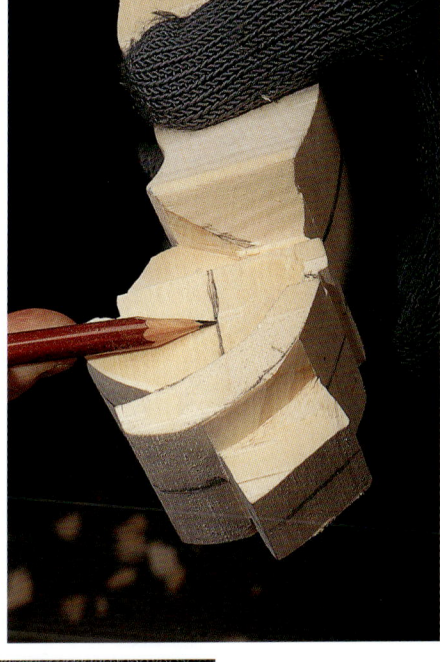

Using a finger as a depth gauge, measure the finished side…

The chin and collar line begin to take shape.

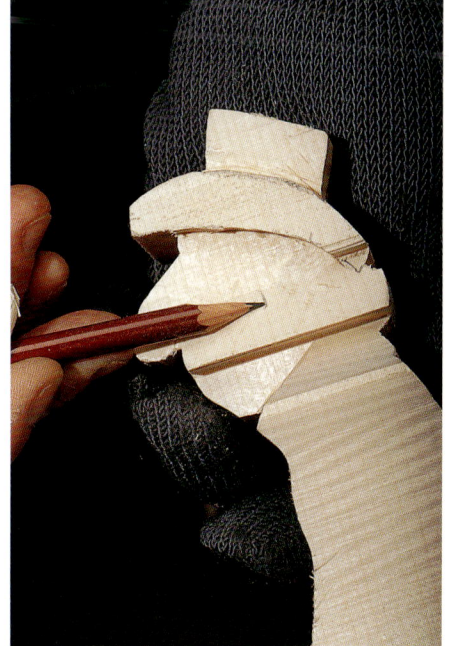

and transfer it to the other side.

Make a mark on each side of the center line to mark the width of the tip of the nose. This can be as narrow or as wide as you want.

Follow the contour of the blank.

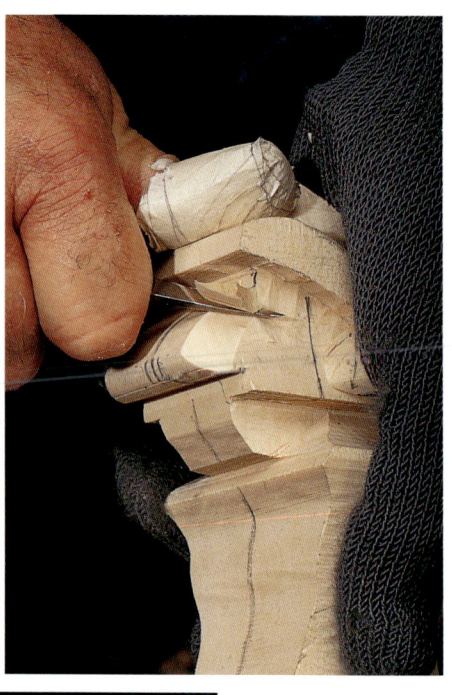

Under the brim of the hat I am going to remove everything from the center side line to the side of the tip of the nose to create a flat surface. In this case it is about a 45 degree angle.

Trim off the chip under the hat brim.

Starting under the nose, use a knife to carve off the excess.

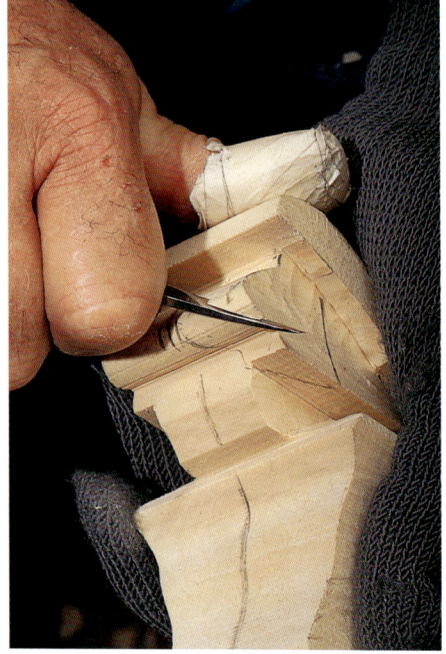

Continue until the surface is established.

Knock off the corner of the lip and jaw, down to the chin.

Progress. Repeat on the other side.

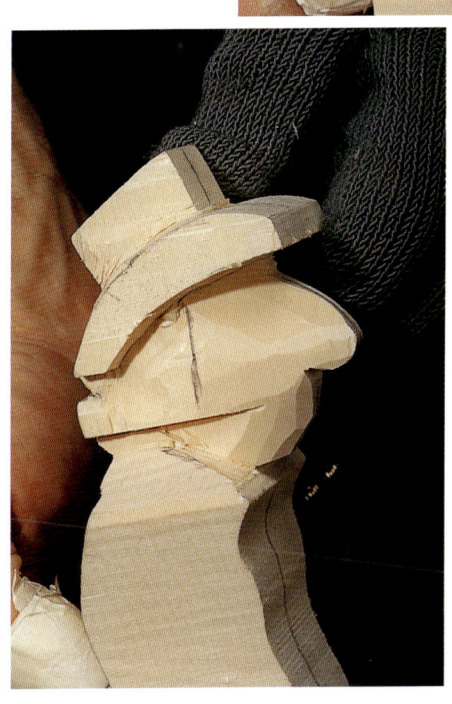

The result. From the bottom you can see the angle.

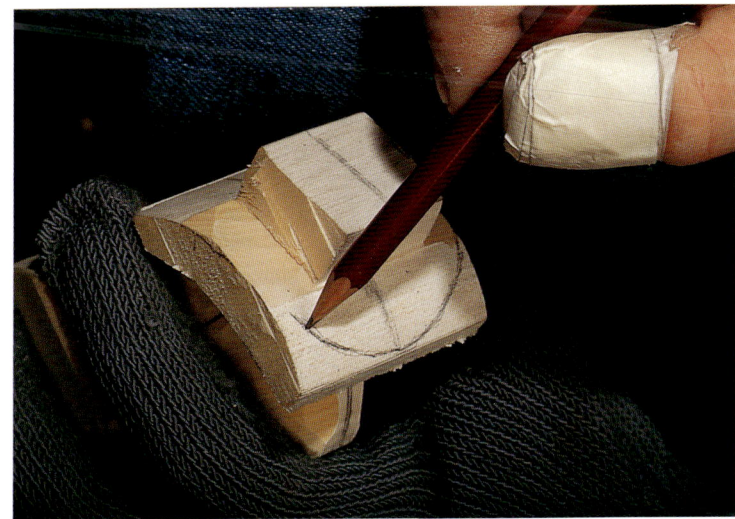

Mark the shape of the brim. I don't finish carving the brim until later, but it helps to get the wood out of the way.

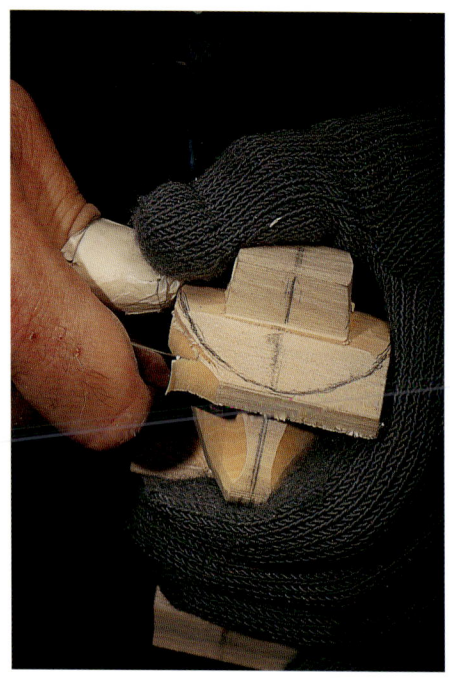

I use a #3, 3/4" gouge to rough out the shape of the brim in the front.

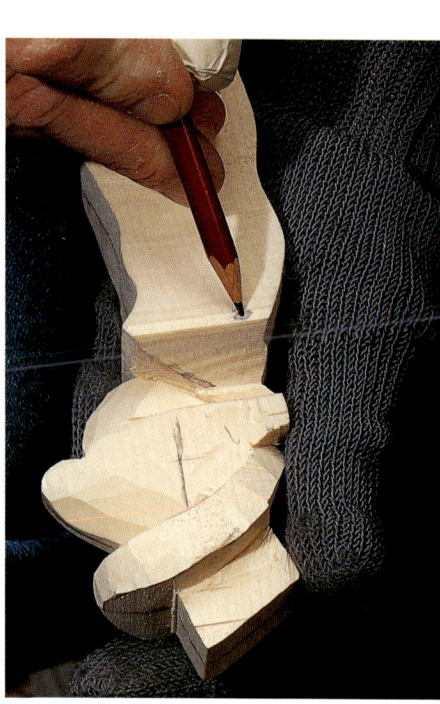

Before trimming the body I need to determine the location of the shoulder joint. In a relaxed person it lines up with the back of the neck. Many carvers make the mistake of moving this joint to far forward, giving their carvings a "Marine-chest" look.

In the back I use a knife to trim the brim.

On the front of the body mark lines on either side of the center line to mark the central flat section of the chest.

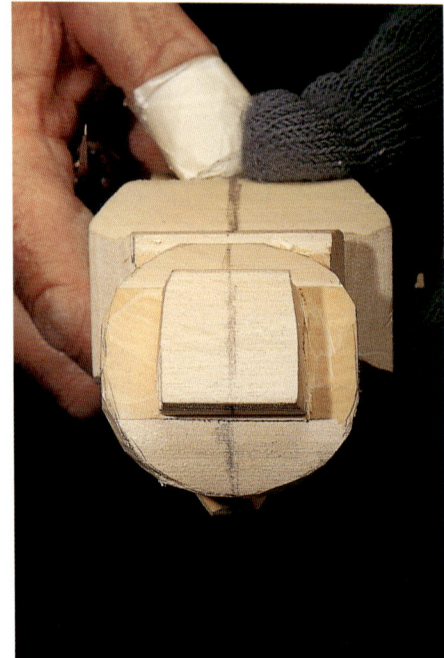

The result.

On the side the line gently flow back to the shoulder socket.

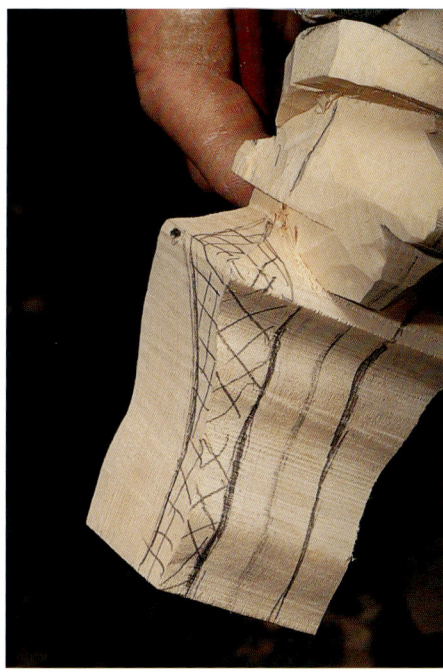

The front edges will be knocked off.

The result.

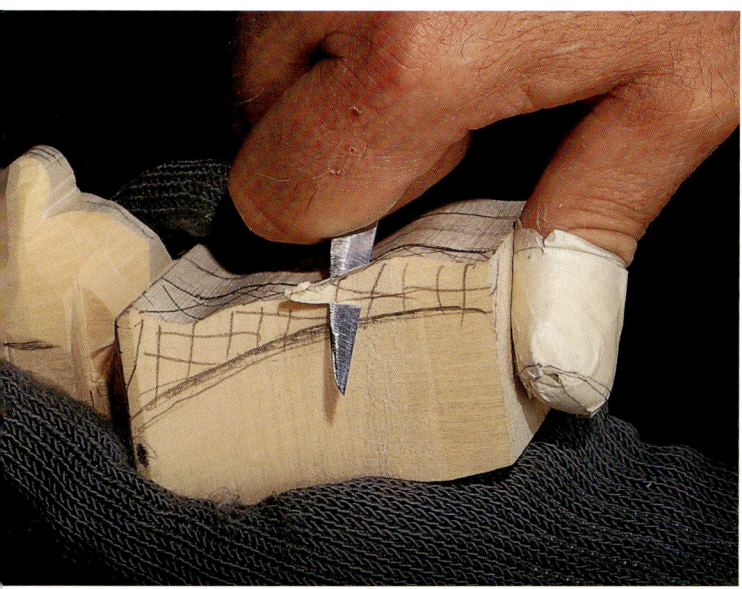

Carve the edges with the knife. Start about halfway and carve away from your body.

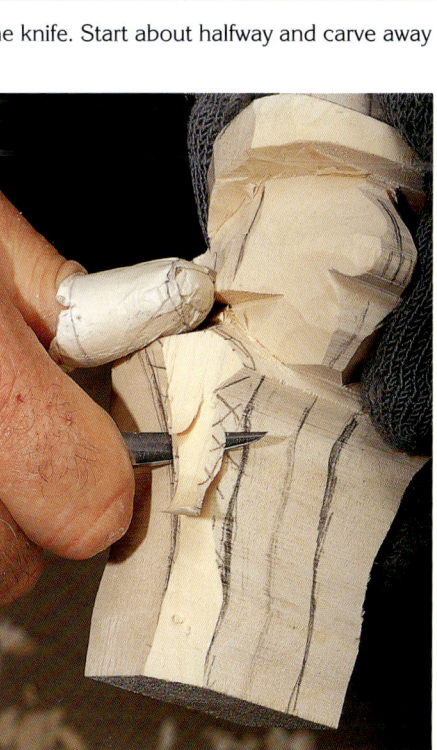

Turn the piece and start halfway again to complete cut. This helps both with safety and grain direction.

I like to clean up sharp edges. On the back, start at the center and knock off the edge.

Turn the piece and work in the other direction.

Continue up into the back of the shoulder.

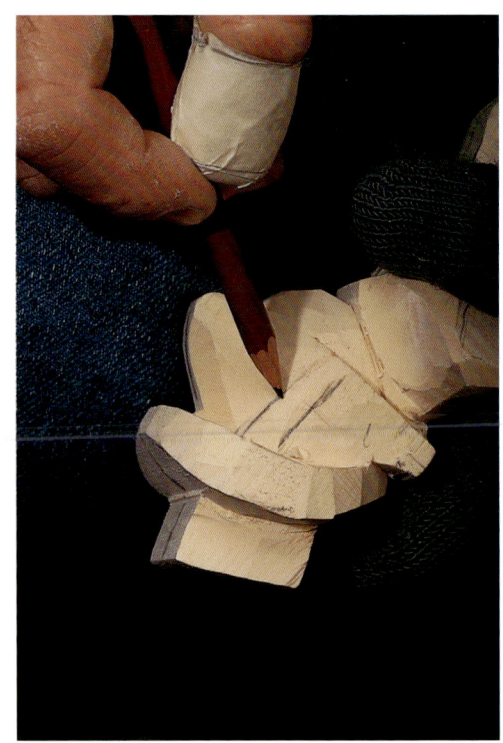

Draw in the front of the sideburn and carry the same line to the other side.

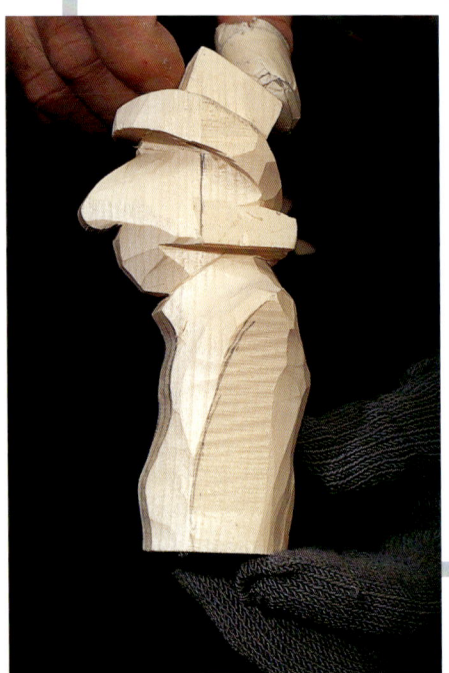

Progress

Below: To narrow the width of the face I use a gouge and knife. With a Swiss #11/3mm gouge I start just above the top of the cheek bone and follow in front of the sideburn line all the way up to the hat.

Do the same thing coming down from the middle. Continue to the bottom of the sideburn.

Bevel the surface of the sideburn so the front edge is almost down to the face.

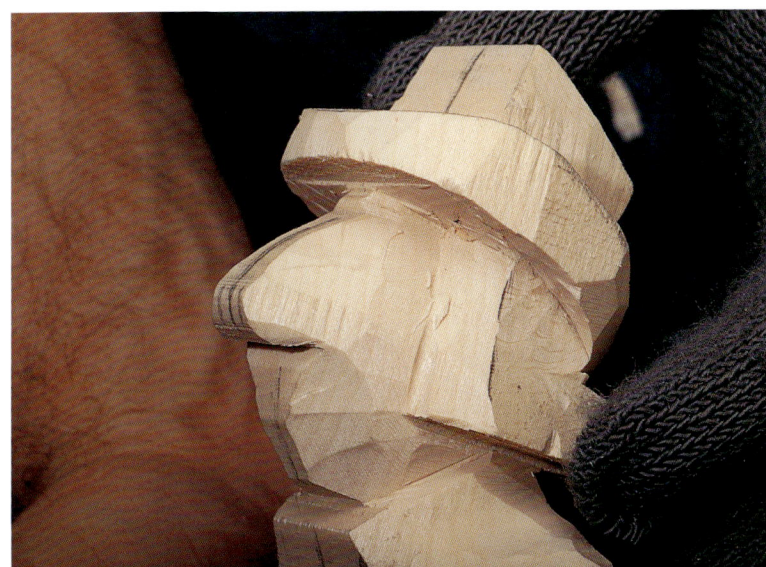

The result.

Thin the face along the gouge line.

Next I establish the angle of the eyes. The slant slightly down from the bridge of the nose.

To begin creating an eye area we cut straight in on the angle.

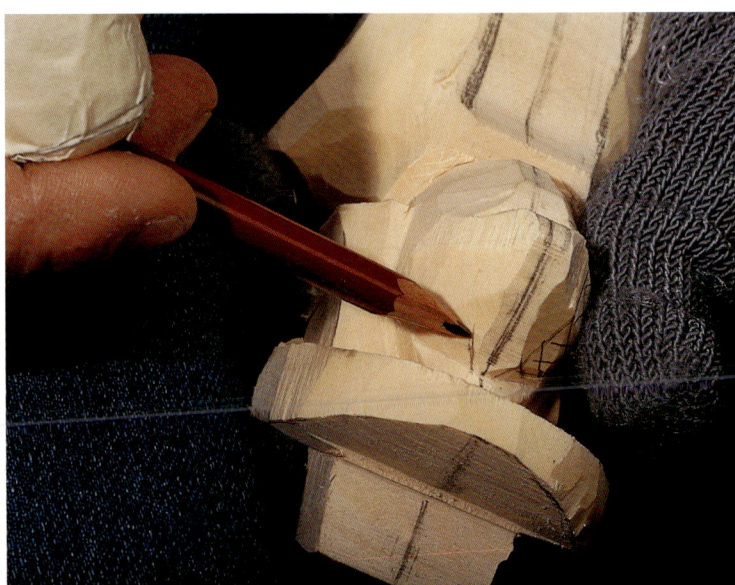

A scooping cut will create planes of the nose and mouth, and pushes back the cheek bone. The area to be gouged starts at the bridge of the nose.

Cut back to the line from the brim.

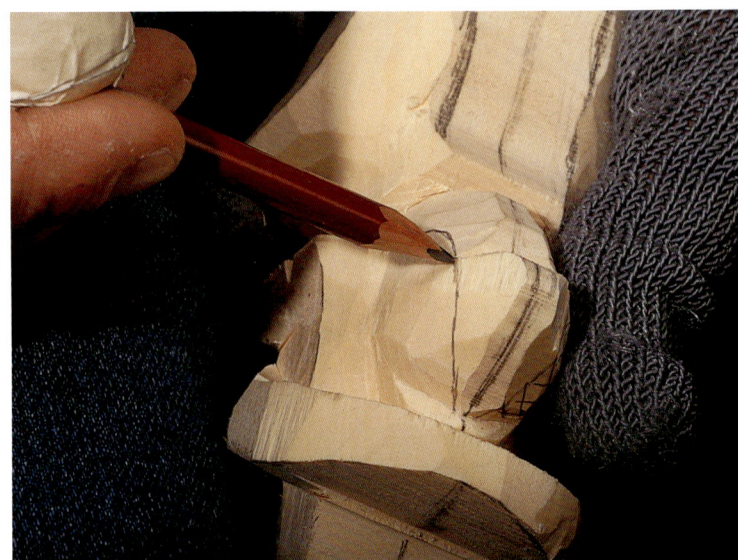

It continues to the back of the nostril…

The result. Repeat on the other side.

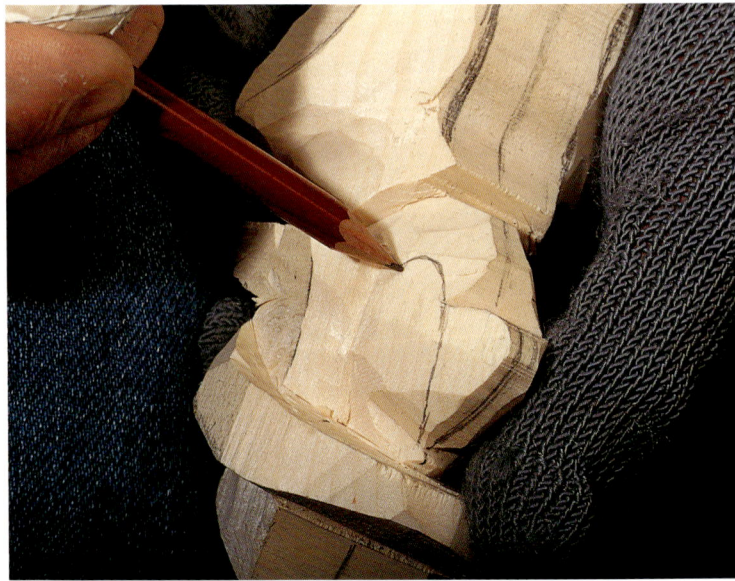

and down into the center of the mouth.

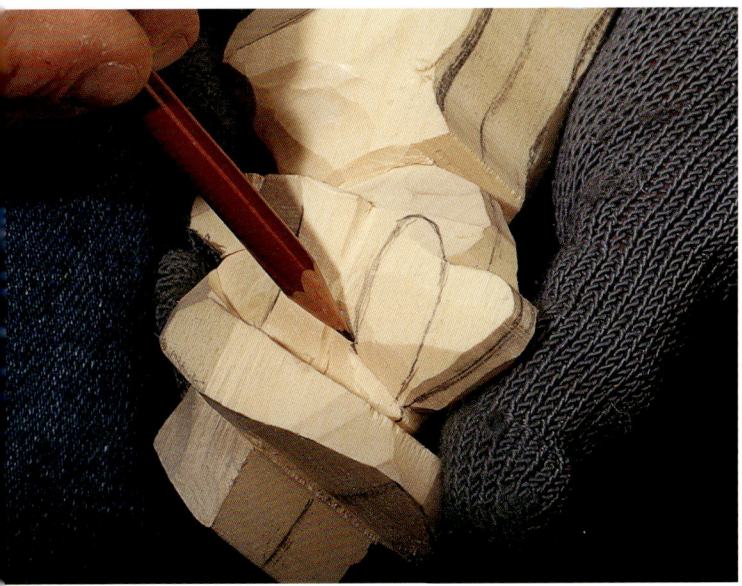

It returns back to the outside corner of the eye.

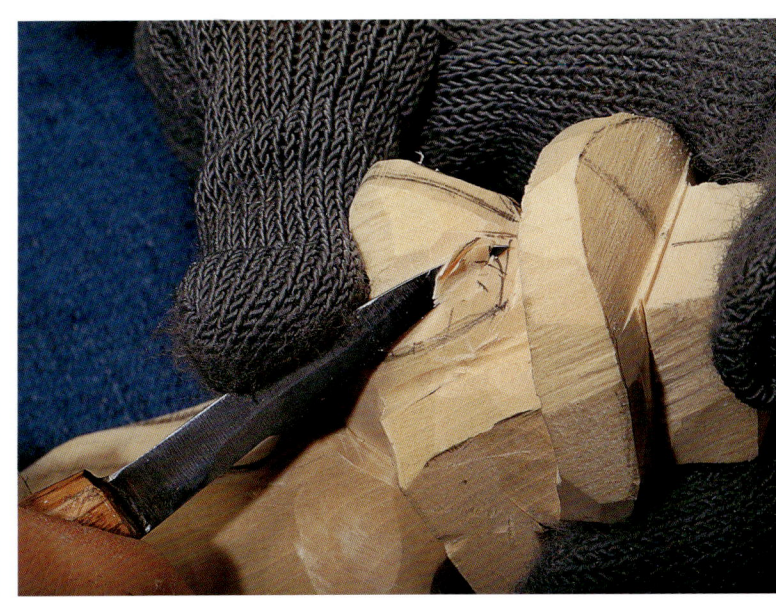

Next work the top of the area, coming almost to the eye area.

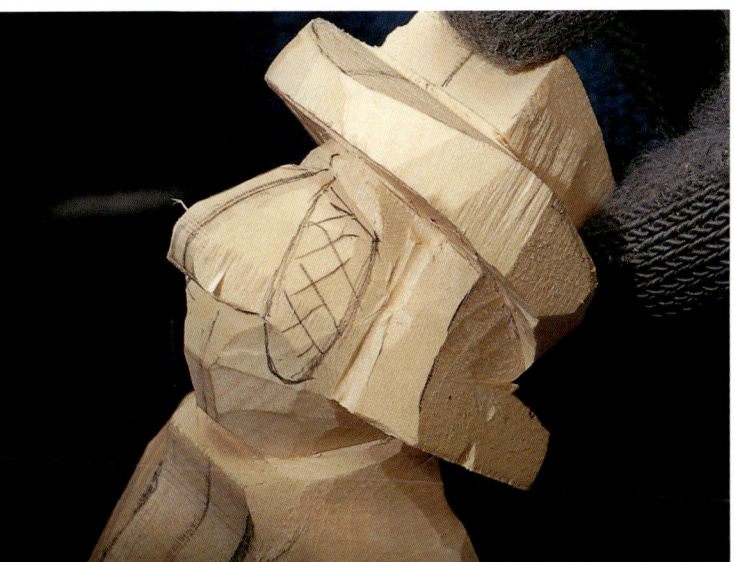

The area to be gouged.

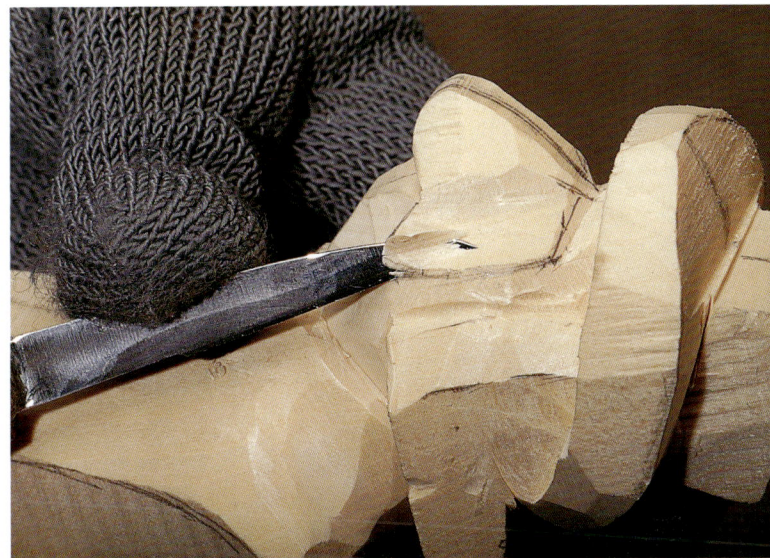

Then move to the bottom of the cut and scoop it out.

You can use a knife for the cut. Start at the front line at the center and scoop back.

If you use a gouge, start again in the center.

Work up to the eye…

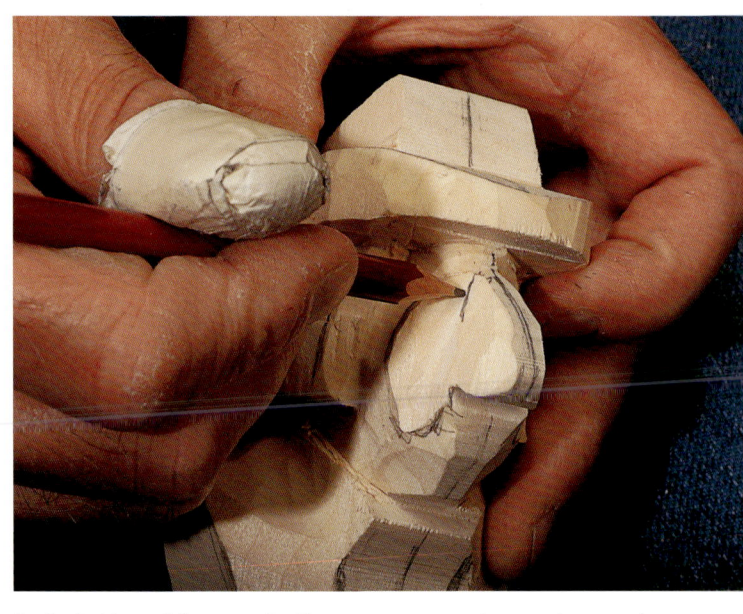

At the bridge of the nose I will use a gouge to deepen the set of the eyes. It will more or less follow this line.

then turn the work and work down toward the mouth.

Cut from the cheek up to the eye. Repeat on the other side.

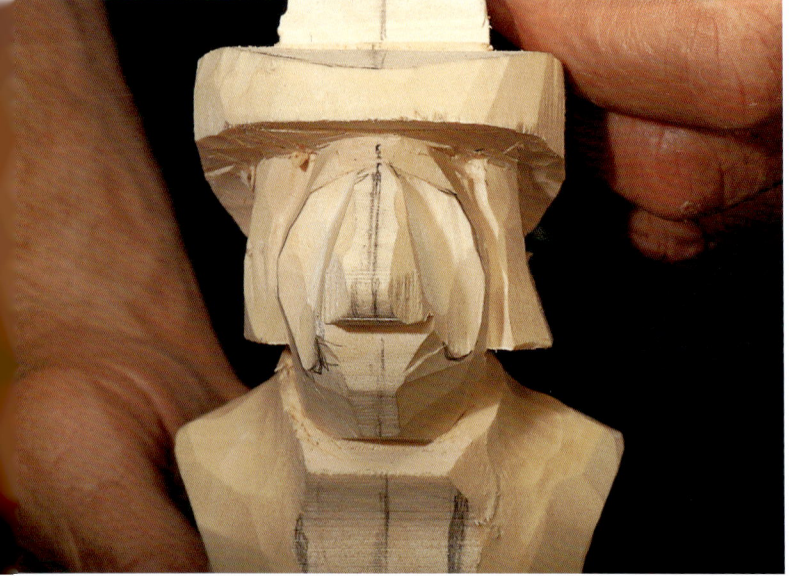

The result.

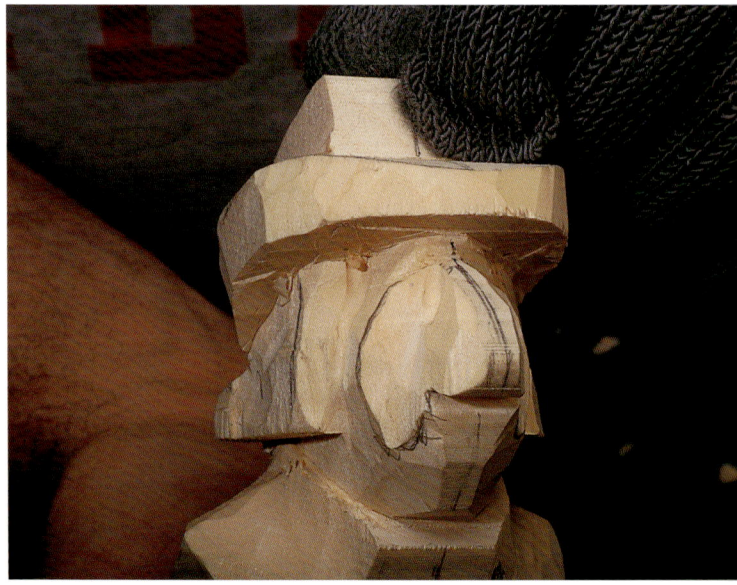

The result.

Draw a line from the outside corner of the eye straight in to the nose.

Make a light stop cut along the eye line, working from the nose outward.

Do the same on the other side. If they align correctly, you avoid the problem of having one eye higher than the other.

With the knife almost flat against the eye area cut back between the nose cut and the eye cut, creating an eye surface.

Make a straight in cut along the nose, from the bridge down to the eye line.

The result.

Repeat on the other side for this result.

Start the smile line. This figure is going to be exaggerated to the left, so on the right side the line will go more directly down. Only draw about this much of the line for now.

Bevel off the ridge that is left. The eye area is now prepared for the actual carving of the eye.

On the left, exaggerated, side the smile line flows more horizontally.

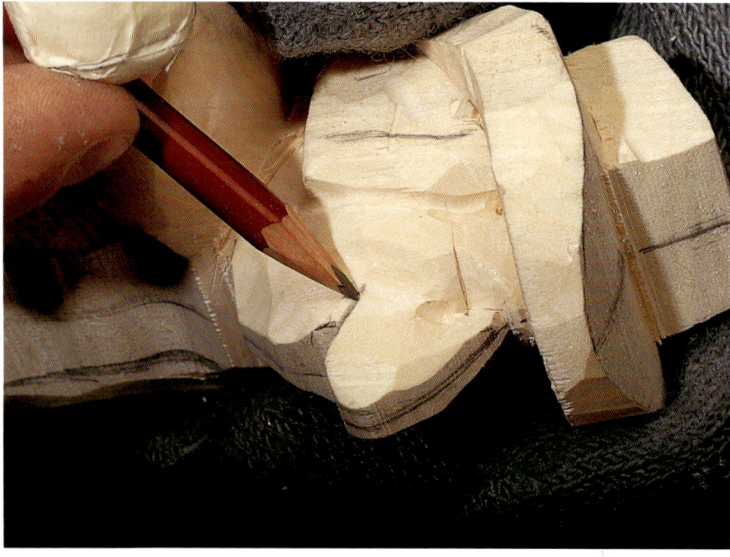

Next we move to the facial expressions. I always determine these before carving the eye. First carry the line of the nose into the face.

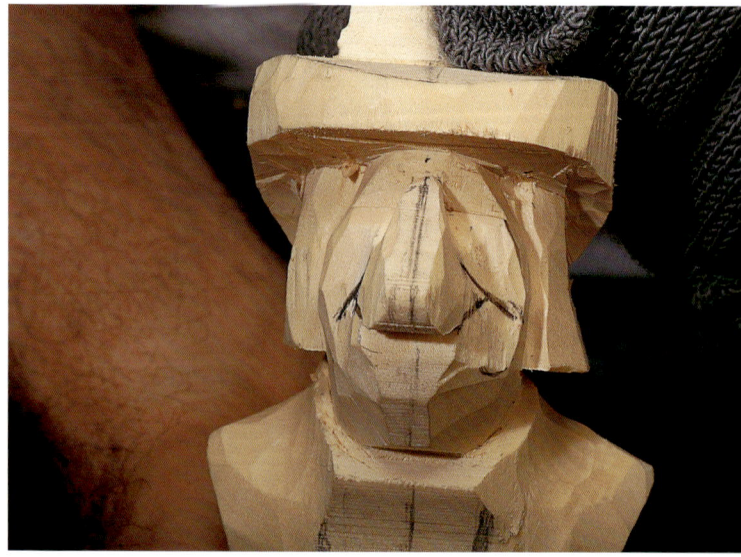

Progress.

Make a stop cut on the smile line. Go over it a couple of time to deepen it.

At the back of the nose, cut a wedge into the smile line.

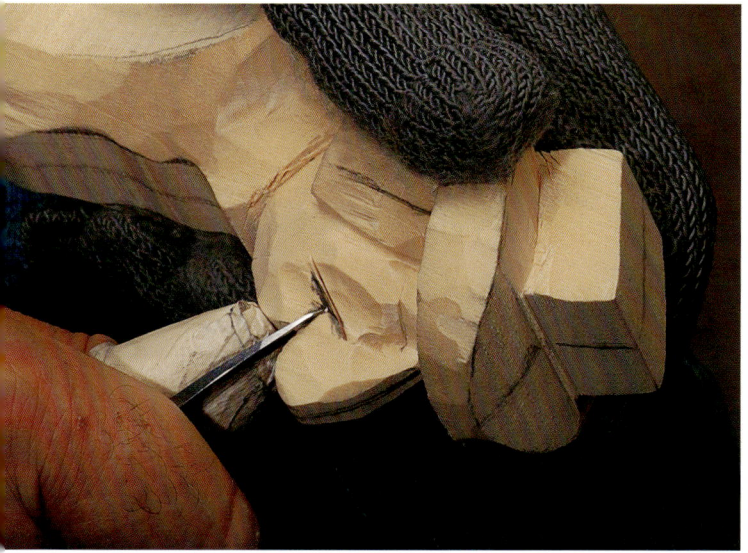

Make a stop cut on the line of the nose.

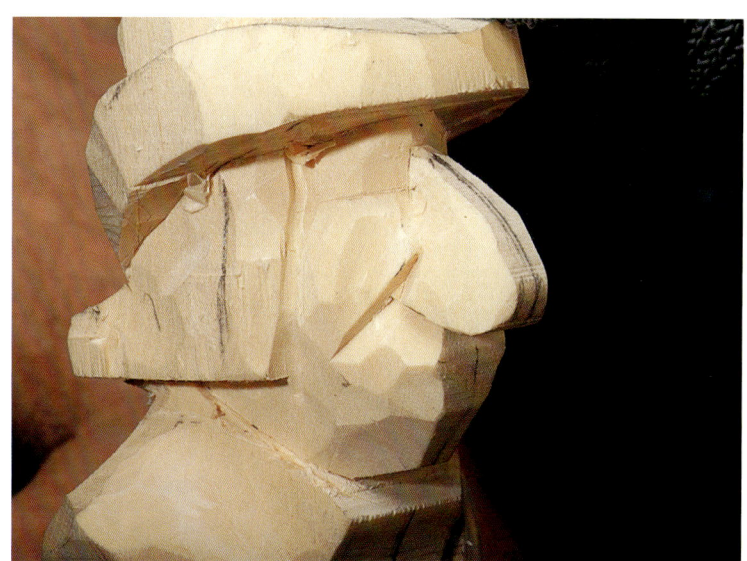

The result.

From the lip shave the area between the stop cuts. Repeat on the other side.

Progress. Before doing more definition to the face, I like to give some form to the rest of the head and neck.

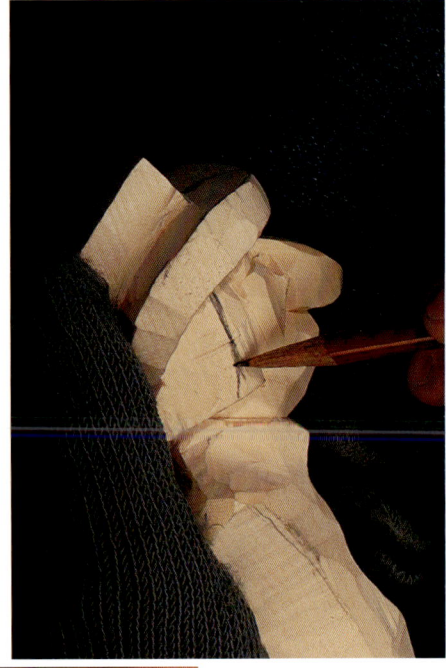

Define the back of the sideburn.

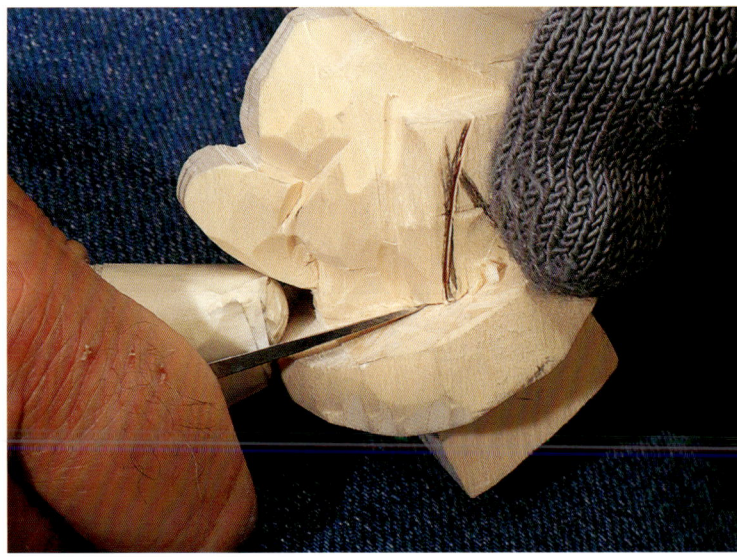

Make another stop at the top of the sideburn under the hat brim.

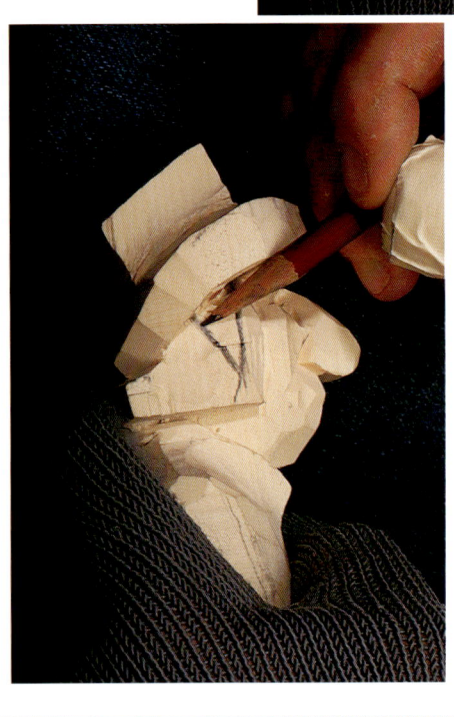

Draw in the back of the ear.

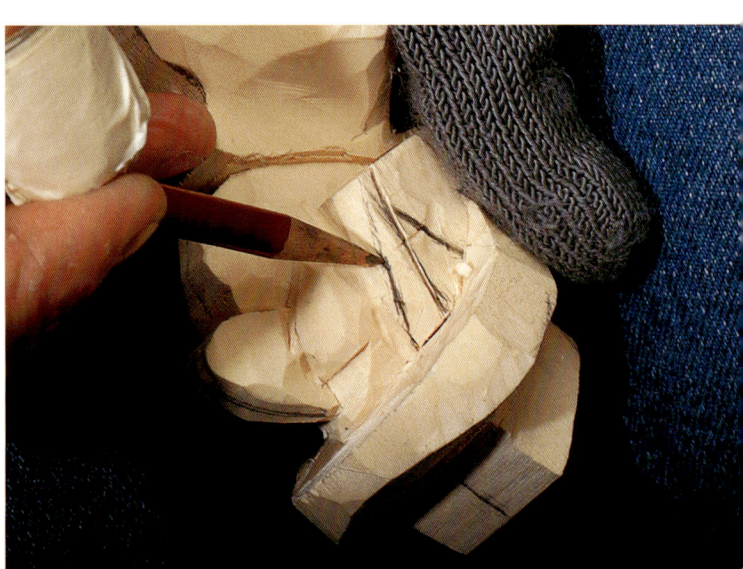

Stock will be removed from the sideburns at an angle so they bush out at the bottom.

Make a deep stop cut on the back of the sideburn.

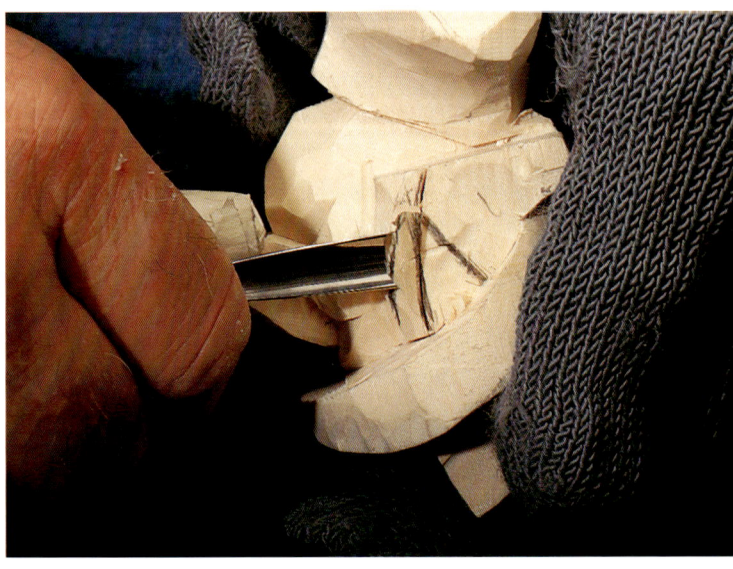

With a Swiss #7/8mm gouge, I push from the front of the sideburn along the line, back to the stop cut. The wood pops off.

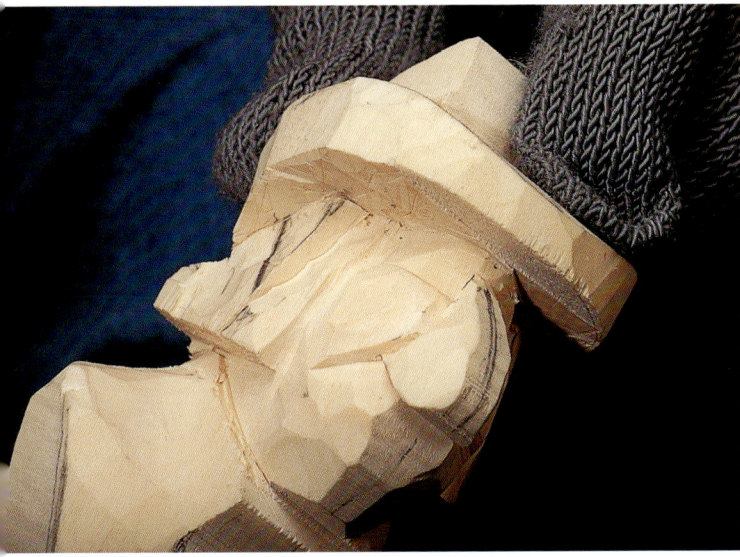

The result. You can begin to see the ear sticking out at the top of the sideburn.

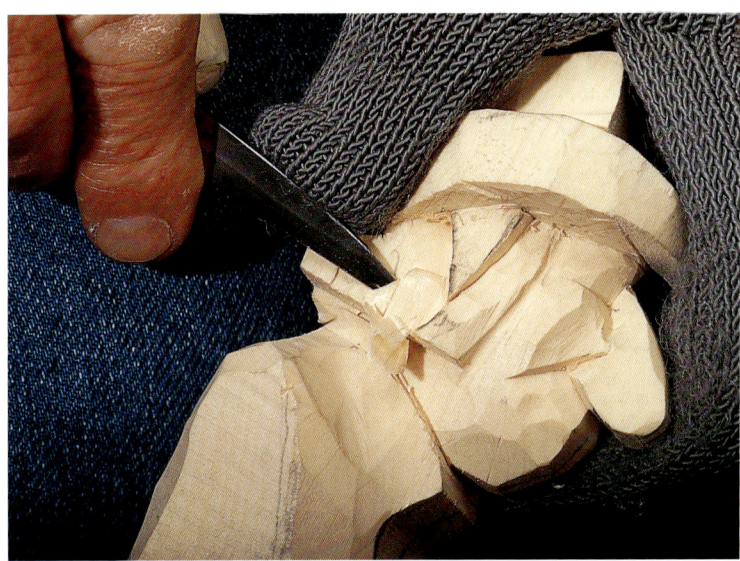

Then take some wood off behind the sideburn. Repeat on the other side.

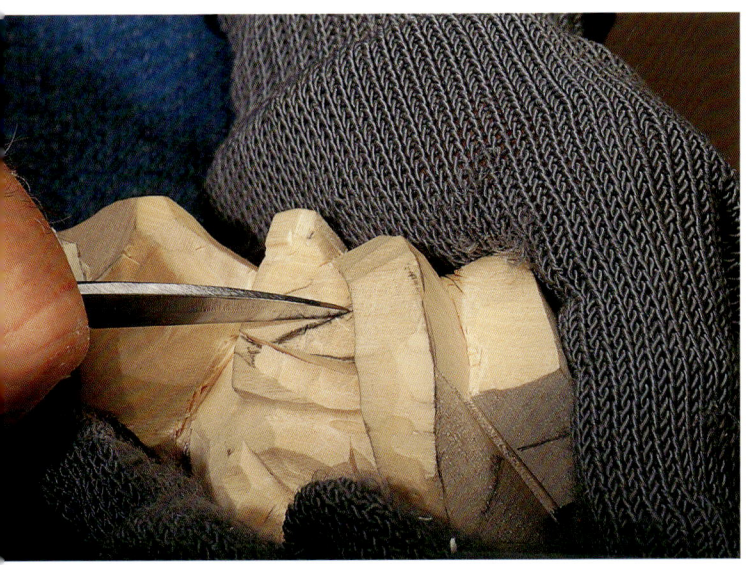

Make a stop cut in the back of the ear.

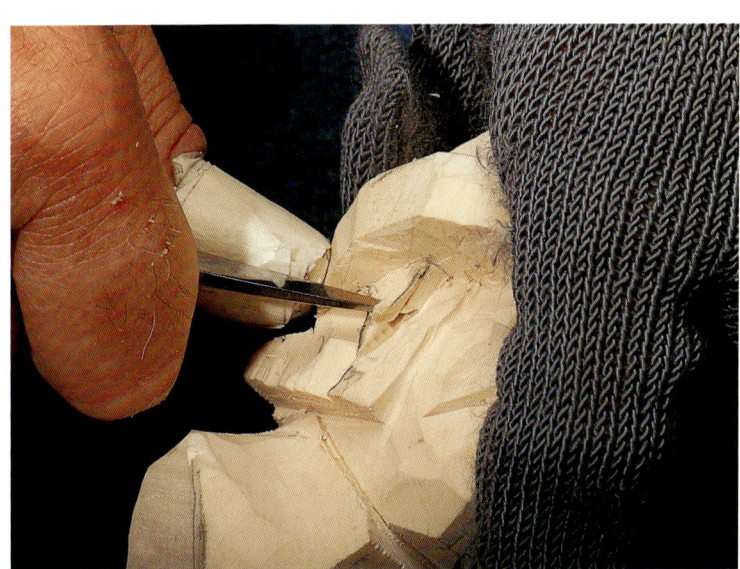

Bevel the surface of the ear down to the level of the sideburn at the front.

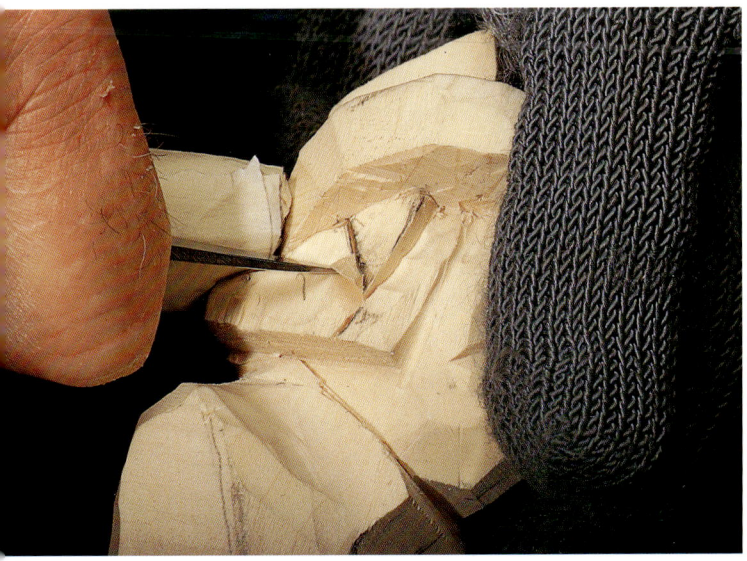

Cut a wedge along the stop cut, from the hair.

Starting about half way up scoop the surface of the ear so it drops behind the side burn.

23

The result.

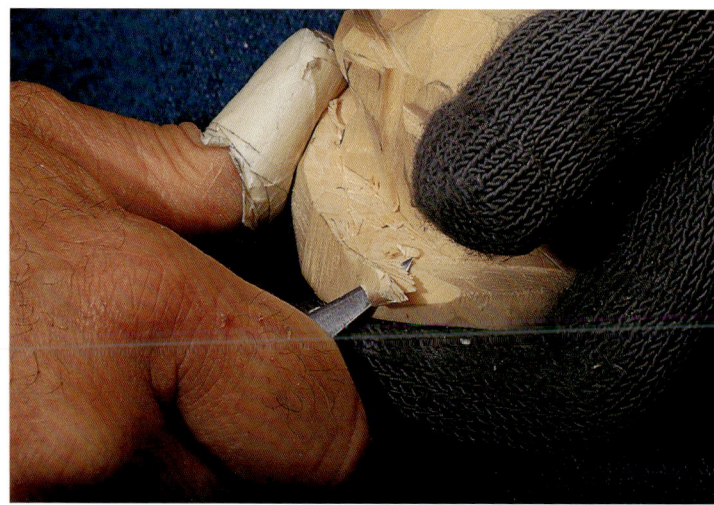

Round up the underside of the brim. This will give better access when we do details on the eyes and ears. I save the final carving of the hat until the end of carving. Too many times have I seen a well-carved hat get knocked off as the carver continued to work.

Begin to shape up the hair, knocking off the back corners.

Progress.

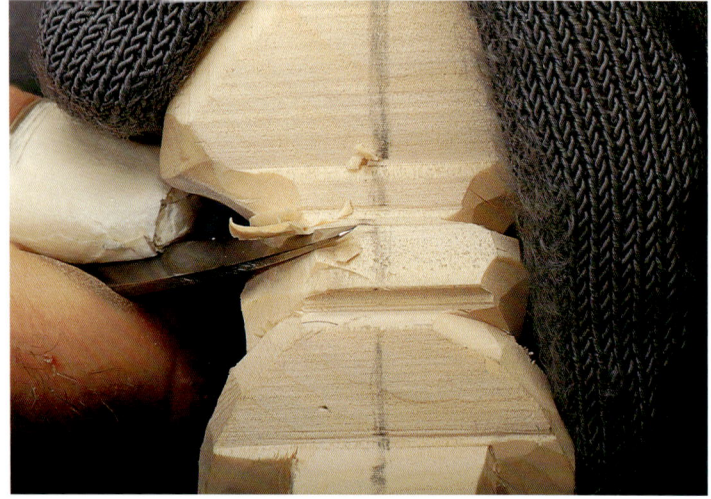

Then make scoop cuts to shape the flow of the hair. These can be kind of raggedy, because that's the way hair is.

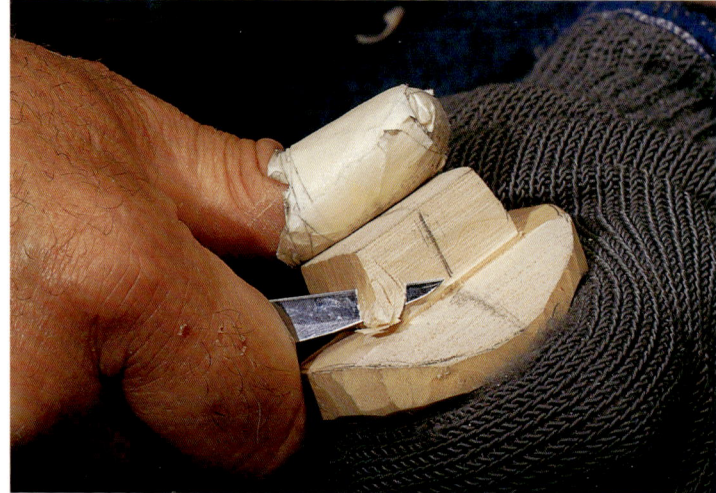

I will also roughly round the crown of the hat. Begin by knocking off the corners.

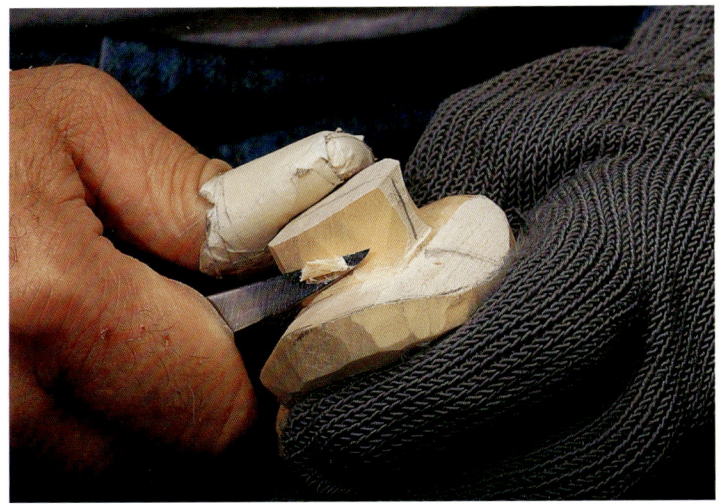

Continue around the crown.

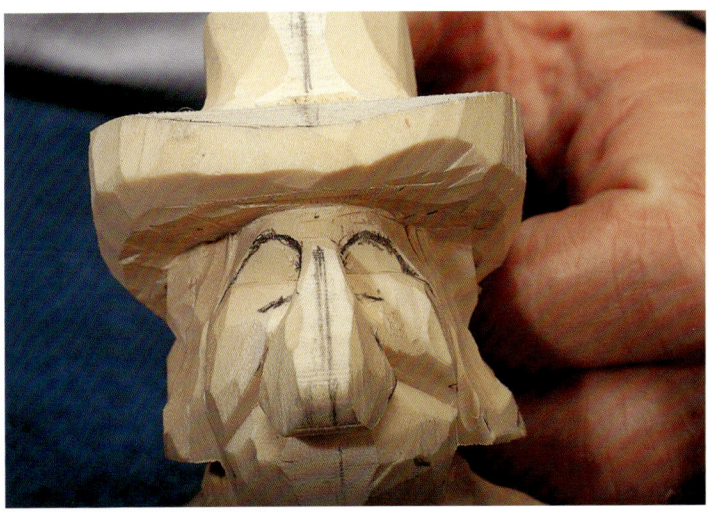

The same procedures are used on the other eye, but because the mouth is exaggerated, the left eye is slightly smaller and more squinty.

Draw the eye socket. Because the left side of the face will be exaggerated and the eye smaller, I work on the right eye first. Start beside the nose and draw the upper arc of the eye socket. Continue down to the cheek.

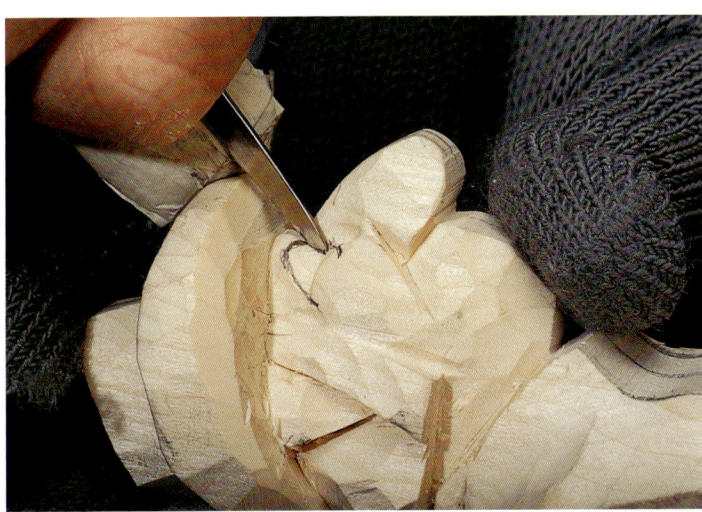

Make a stop cut in the lines drawn for the eye socket. Don't make deep cuts. It is better to make three or four shallower cuts because you are going across the grain most of the way.

Come back and draw the lower line of the eye socket.

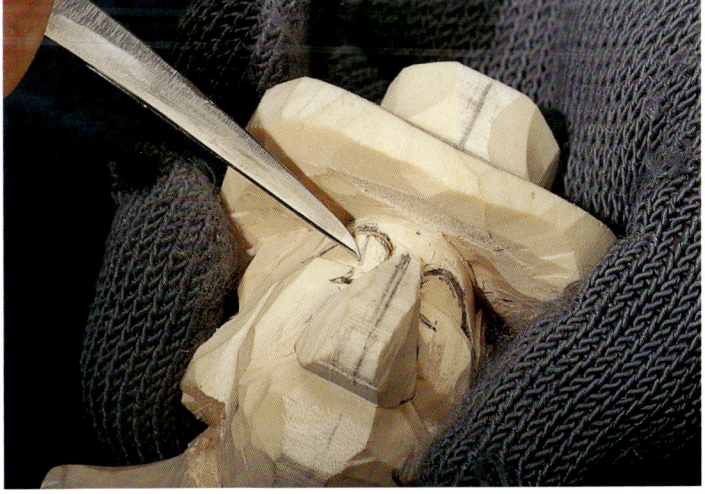

On the inside third of the eye, take a wedge out.

Carve along the surface of the eye to the stop cut.

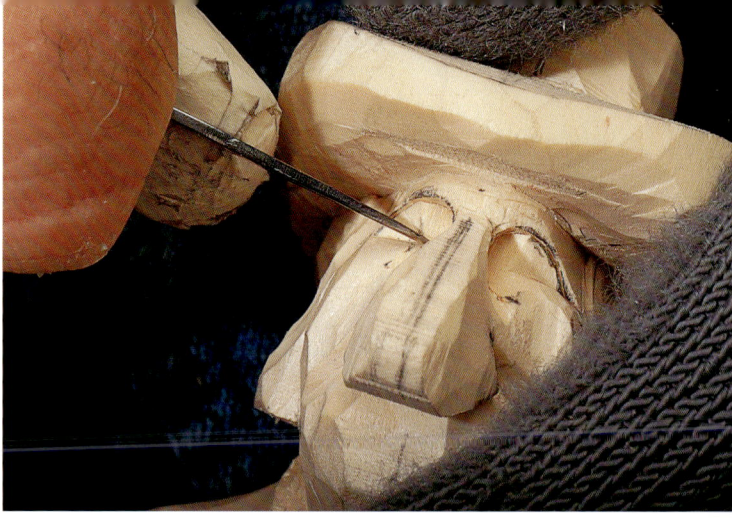

Scribe the line with the knife on both sides.

The result. This establishes the inside curvature of the eye.

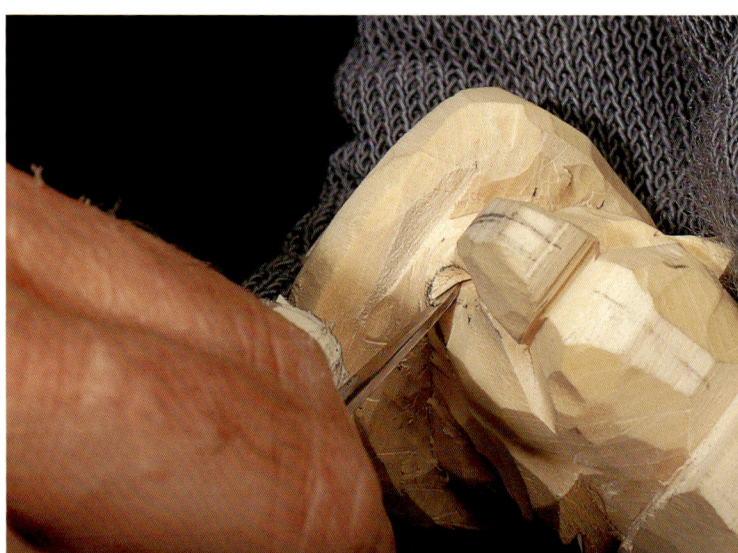

To form the eye mound I cut three wedges from the top and one from the bottom. The first is in the upper corner next to the nose. Place the blade flat against the surface and cut into the socket stop cut made earlier.

With the second eye complete we need to recreate the bottom eyelid, which was lost in the last step.

The next is along the top toward the outside of the eye socket. Again keep the blade against the surface and cut into the socket stop cut.

The third wedge is from the outside corner along the top surface.

Progress.

Finally cut a wedge at the bottom inside corner, starting at the nose and working out.

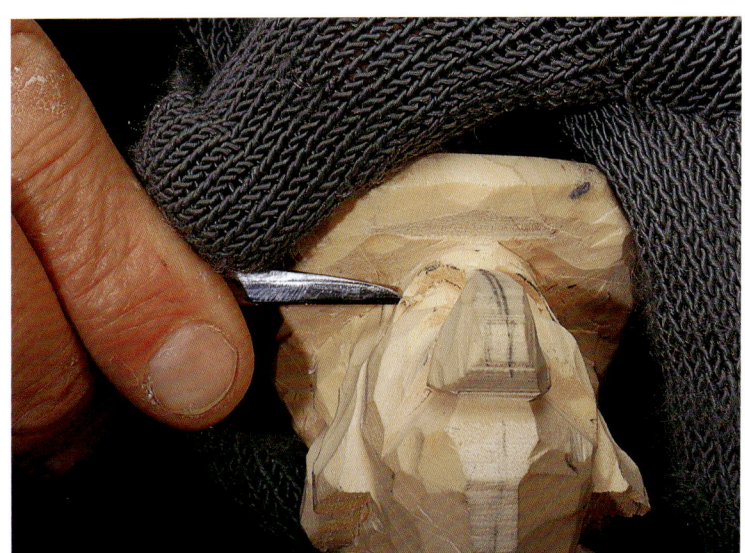

Bevel off the sharp edge of the eyebrow.

This is the rough eye mound. Repeat on the other eye.

With the exaggeration to the left, I need to stretch the right side of the face. Cutting along the jaw will make it longer.

Round off the mouth mound.

The result.

Next I want to stretch the smile line on the right side of the face, making it longer.

Make a pretty deep stop cut right on the expression line.

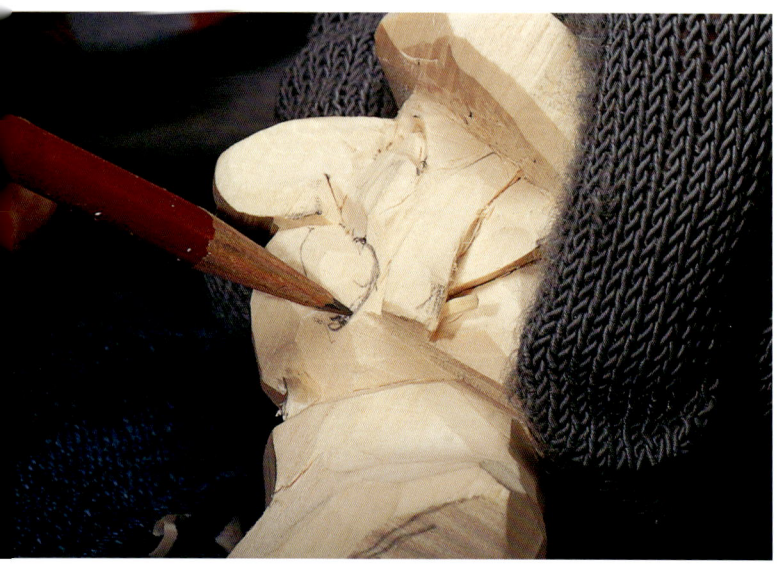

The expression line on the left side is more horizontal, higher and shorter.

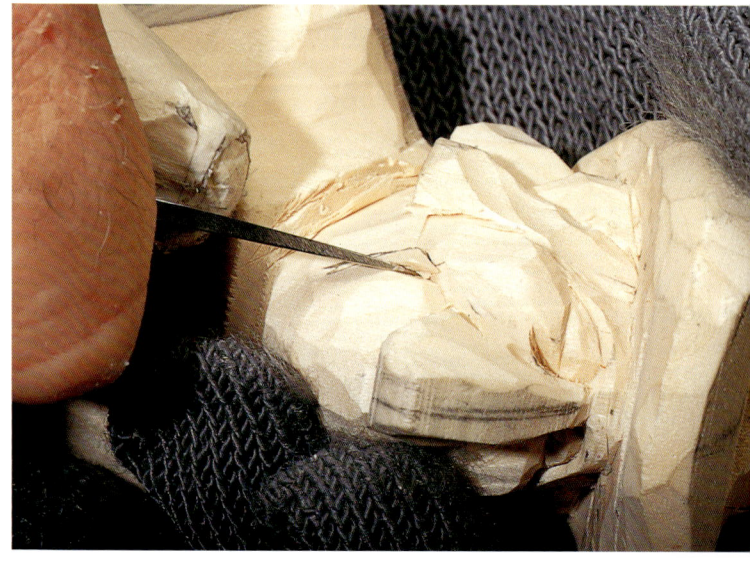

With a slicing cut from the mouth mound, take a wedge out along the expression line

Deepen the cut to raise the cheek. Do the same on the other side.

Cut the wedge out to relieve the wood. With the shoulder in the way this may take some patient carving. Repeat on the other side.

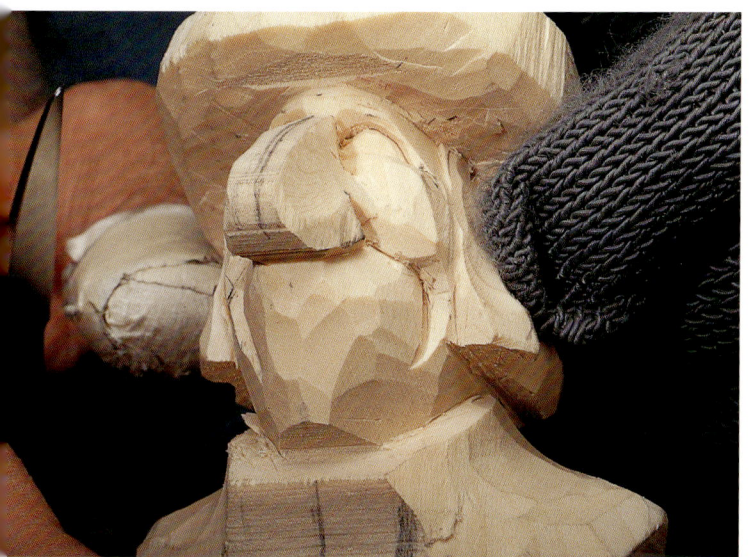

The exaggerated side is cut just a little deeper.

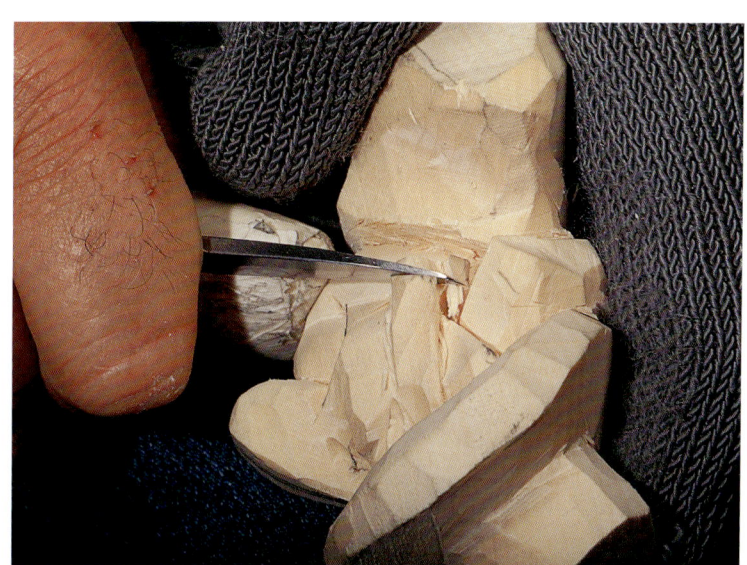

The sideburns are a little longer than they need to be, so I will shorten them. Do the same on the other side.

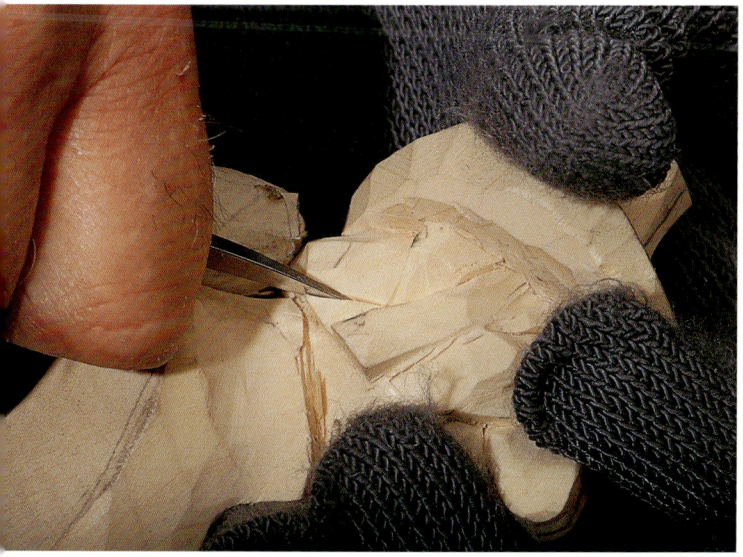

Define the hair line in back of the sideburn at the bottom of the ear. Make a stop cut.

Use a #11/3mm gouge to form the jaw line. It starts under the sideburn at the point where the earlobe would end if you could see it.

With a knife, smooth the transition between the jaw and the neck.

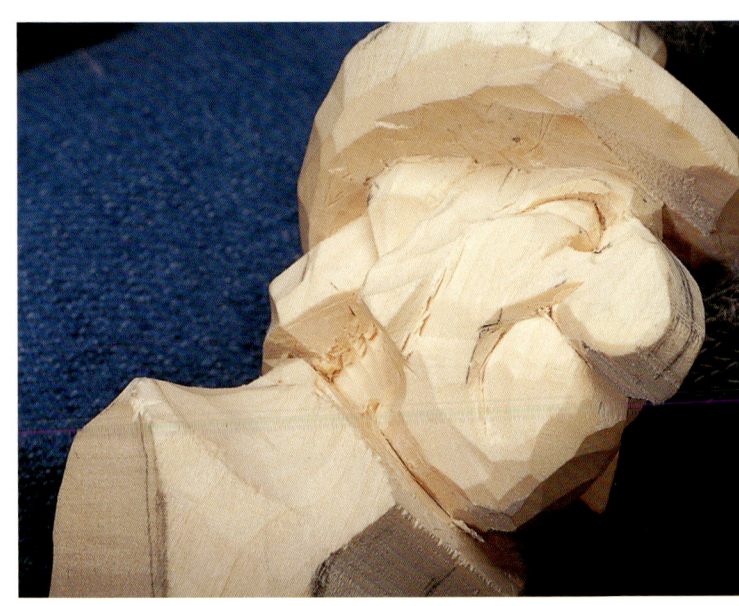

Before doing more with the head, I want to give shape to the body and collar.

Form the jaw with slicing actions toward the chin, using a knife.

Scoop the front of the shoulder so it rises to the collar.

The result.

Continue around the side and the back.

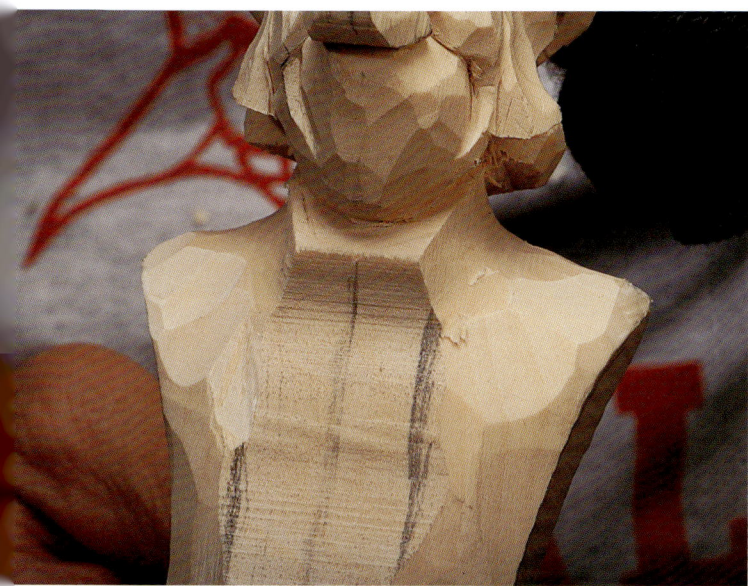

Blend the carving into the body for this result.

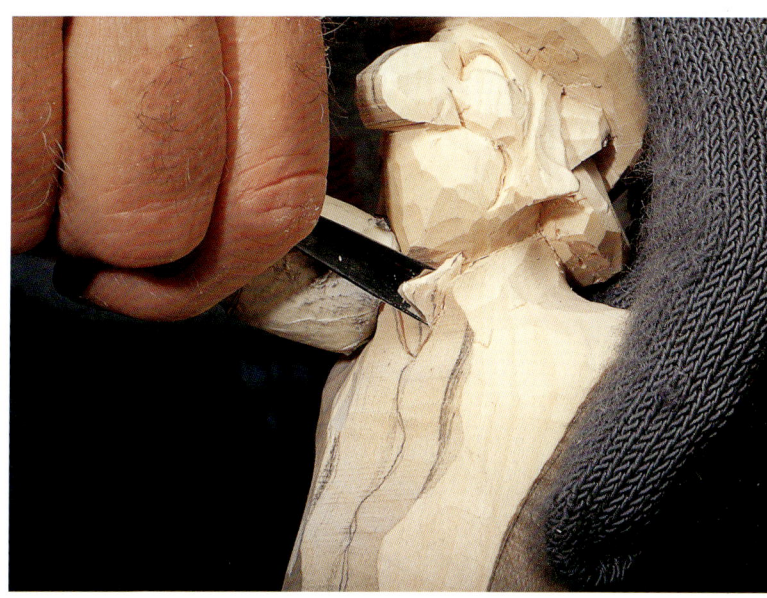

With a flat gouge, remove as much wood from the collar opening as possible.

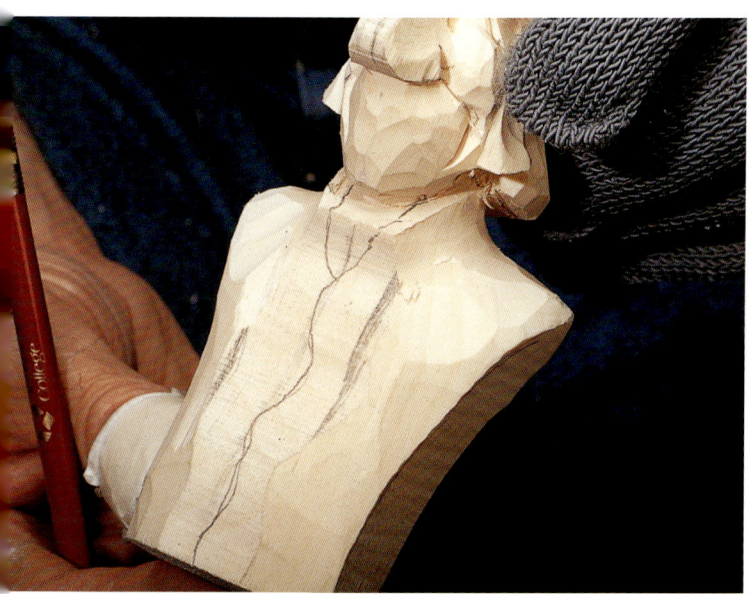

Draw in the opening of the collar and shirt.

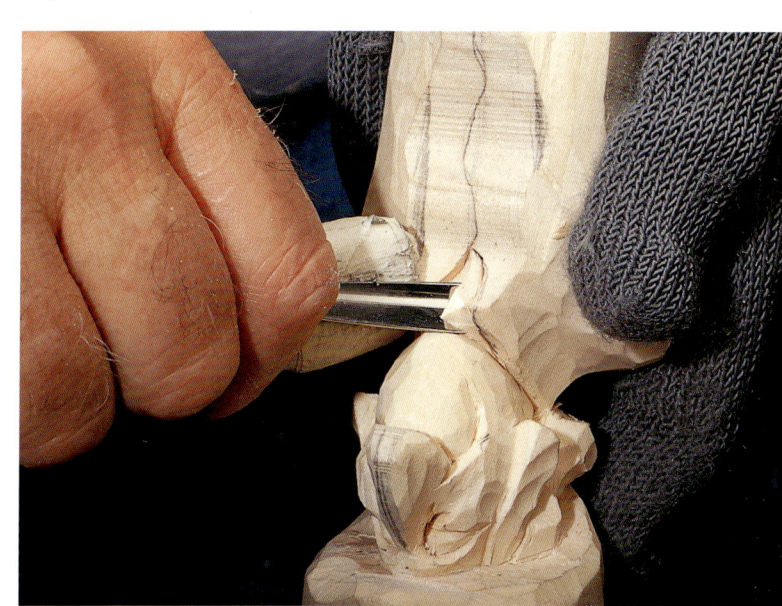

Work from the middle out to the stop cut.

Make a stop cut in the collar line down to the V. Go back and deepen it and repeat on the other side.

The result.

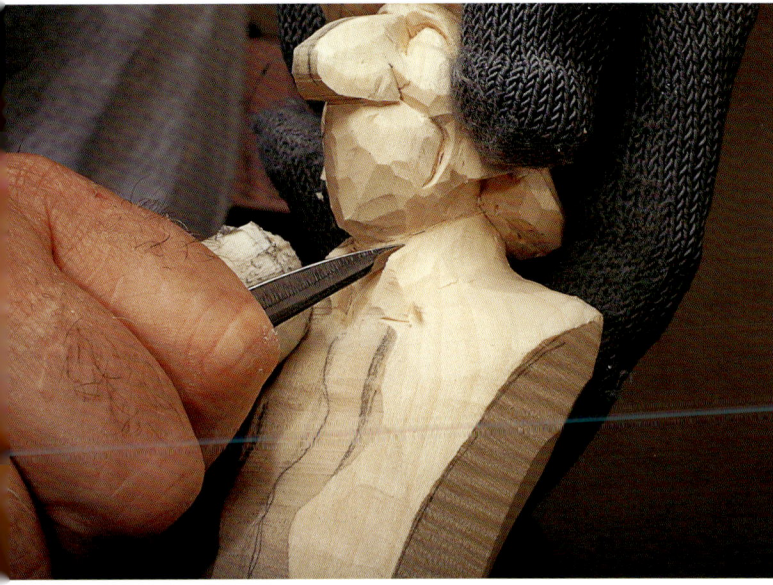

Use a knife to clean up, deepen, and round off the edges.

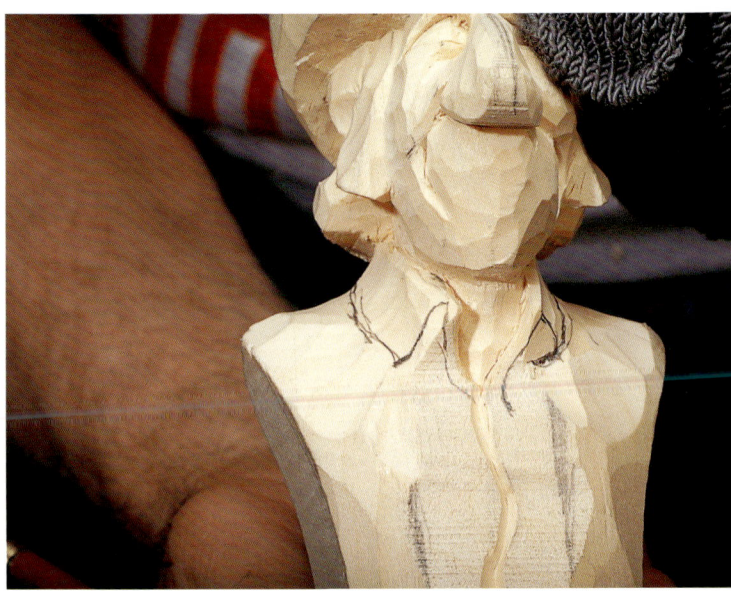

The right collar will lie out like this.

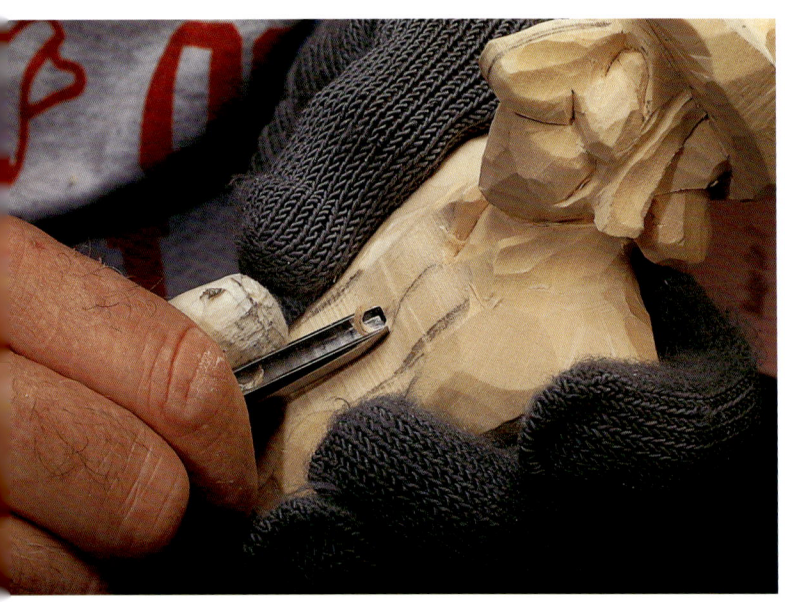

With a v-tool follow the line of the shirt opening.

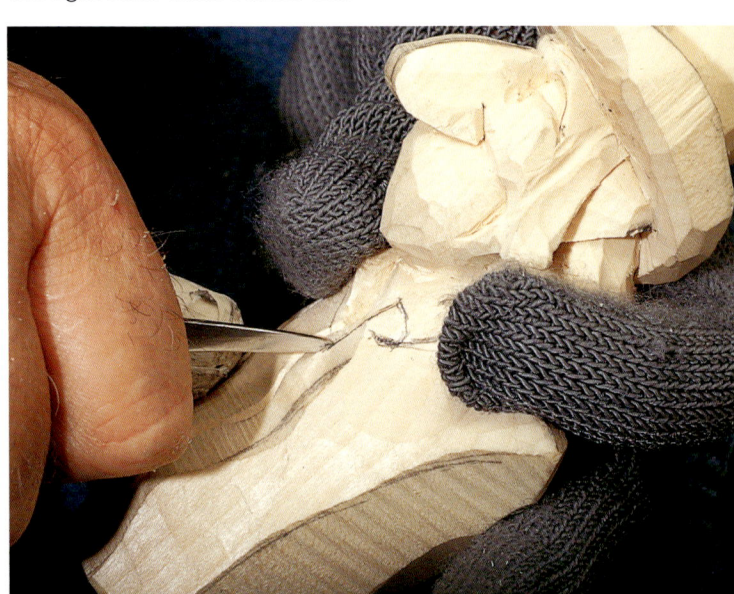

Cut a stop in the collar opening.

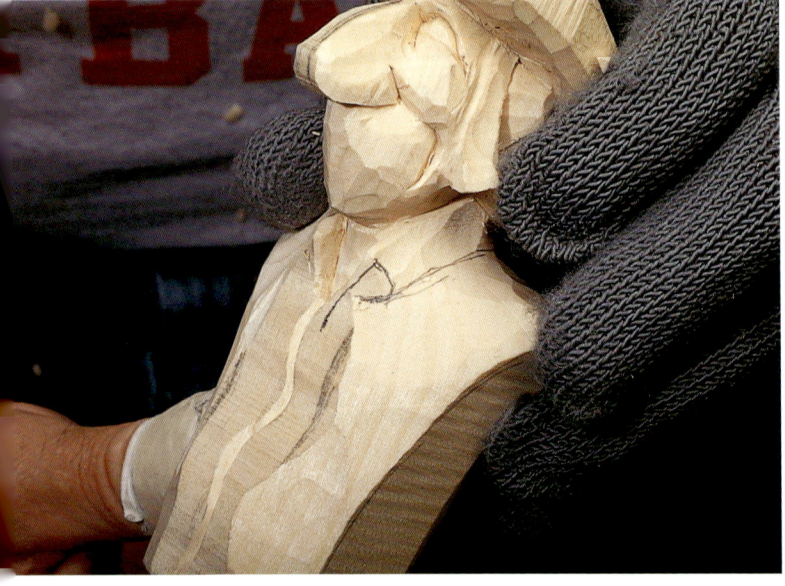

Draw in the collar. On the left, the collar will curl under at the front.

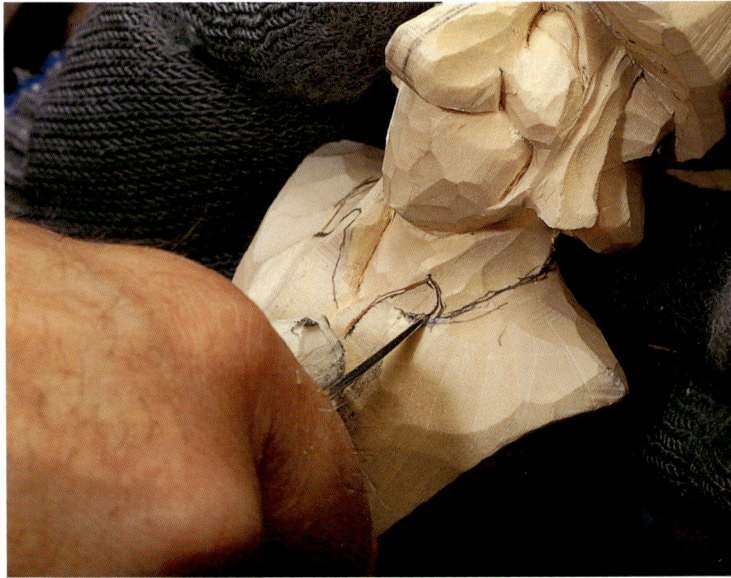

Follow the front edge of the collar around with a stop…

and remove the chip in the middle.

Remove the wedge between and deepen the cuts for this result.

Progress.

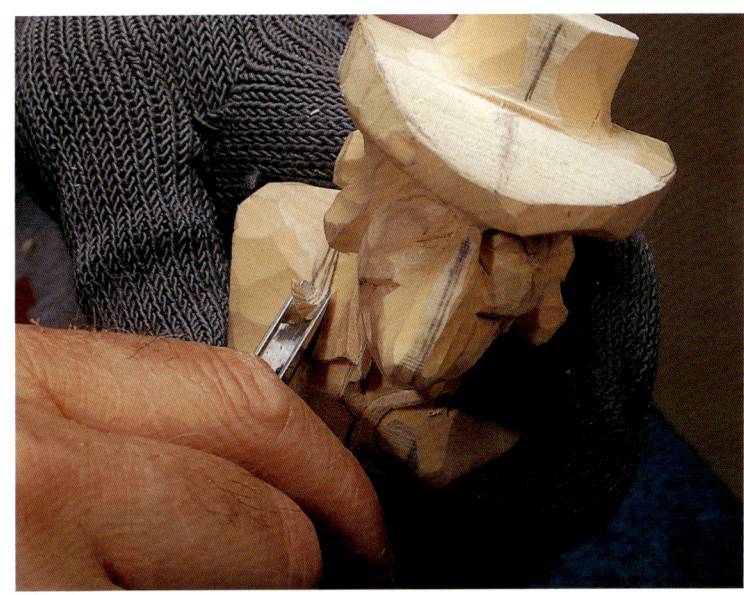

With a v-tool follow the line of the collar around back to the other side.

Do the same on the other side. Make a stop cut on the collar edge and the opening.

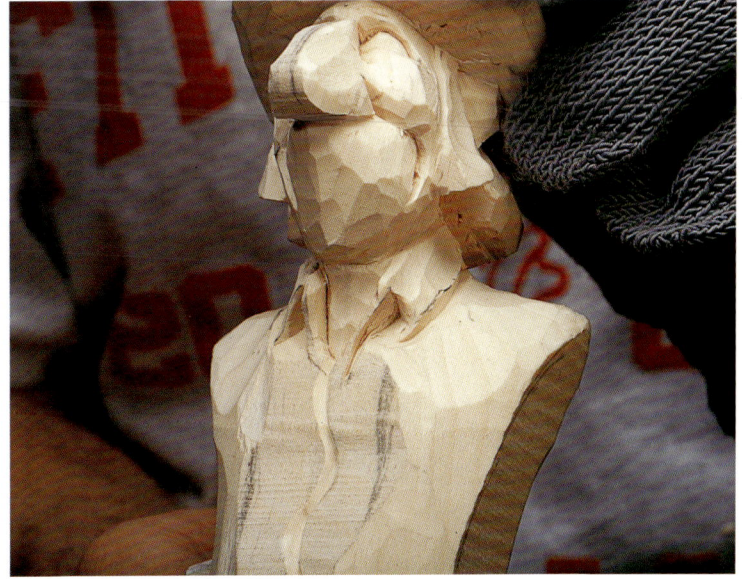

The finished collar.

I like to give my characters broad smiles, even if they are usually a little lopsided. Draw in the mouth line.

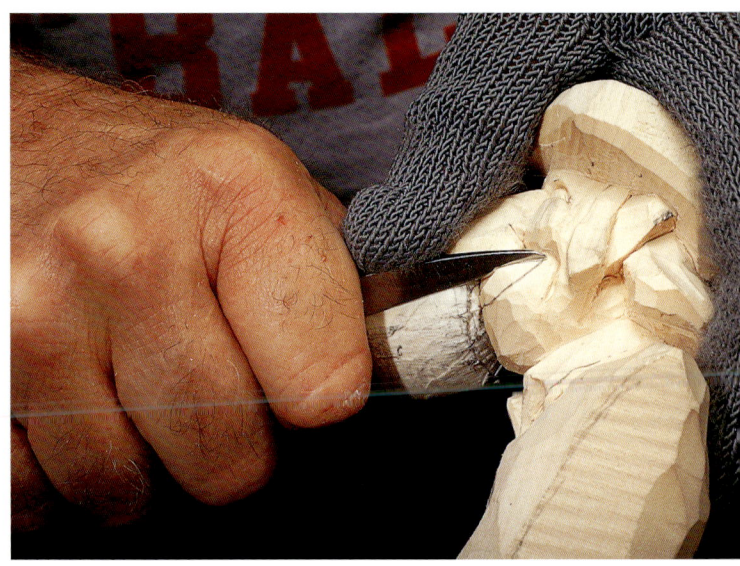

Continue to one corner. Down at a slight angle...

The first cut on the mouth is the top lip at the center. It is not quite straight in.

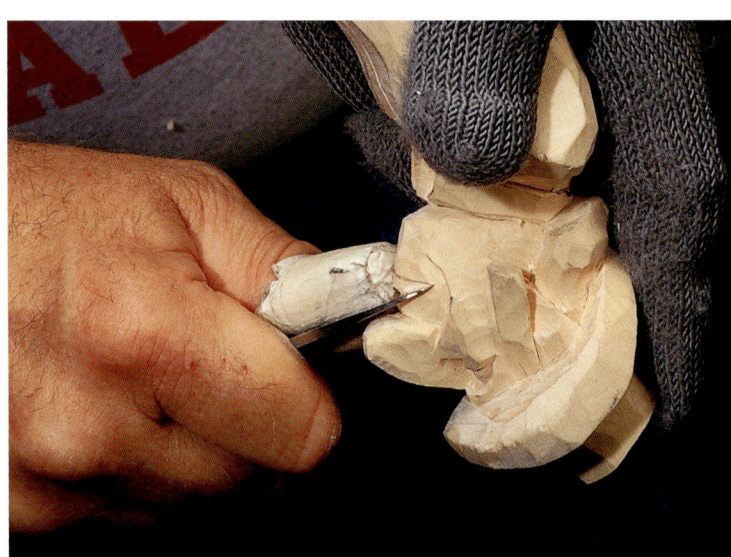

Do the same in the other corner.

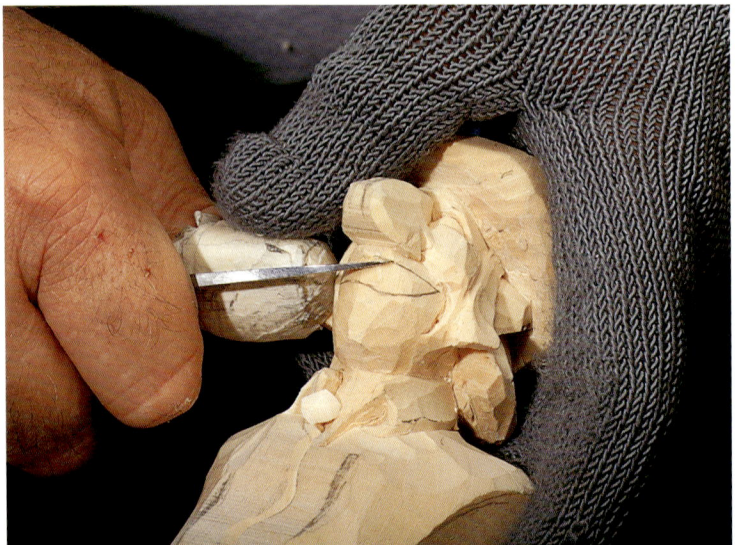

Cut back from the mouth to relieve a wedge. We want the lips to be deep enough that the teeth appear to be behind them.

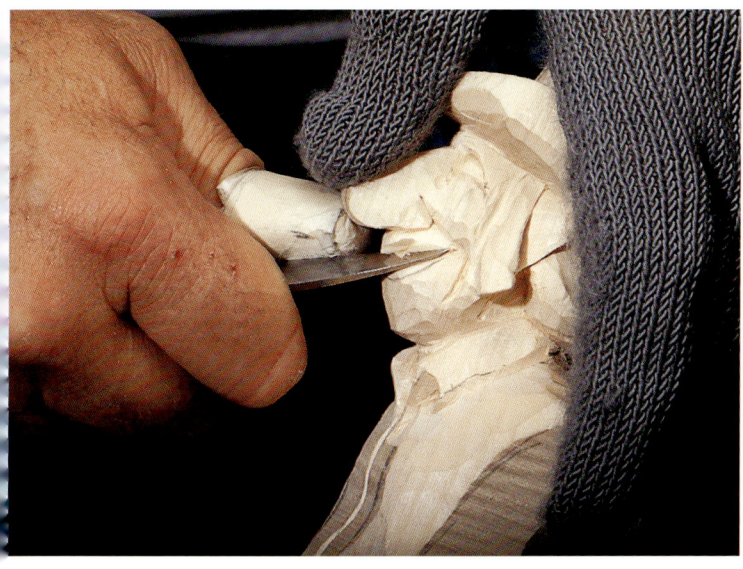

Starting at the line for the bottom lip, bevel the tooth surface up toward the wedge cut below the top lip.

The result.

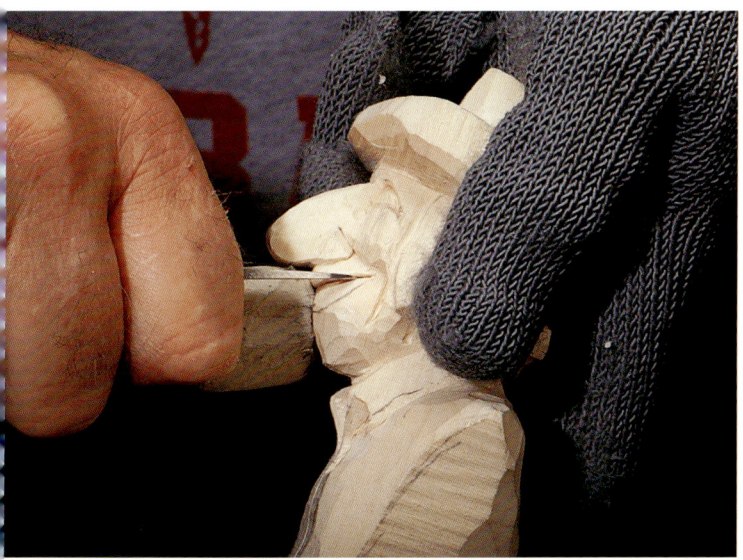

At the corners, undercut the upper lip fairly deeply.

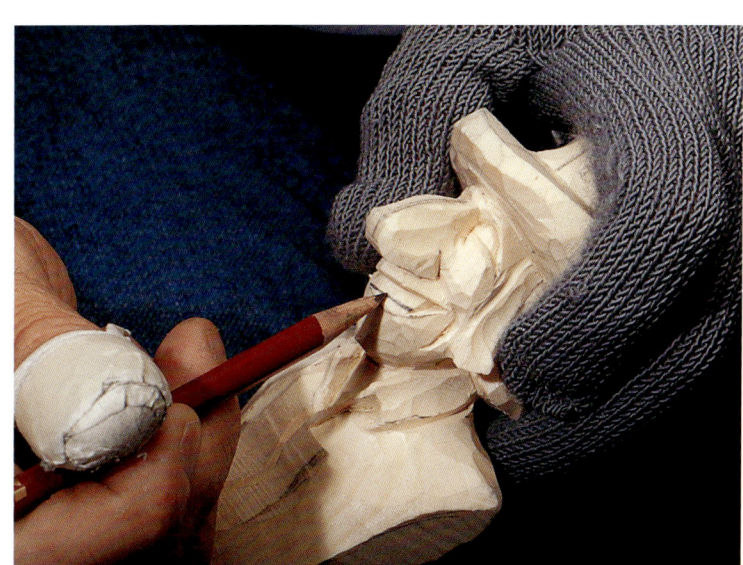

Draw in the bottom of the top teeth.

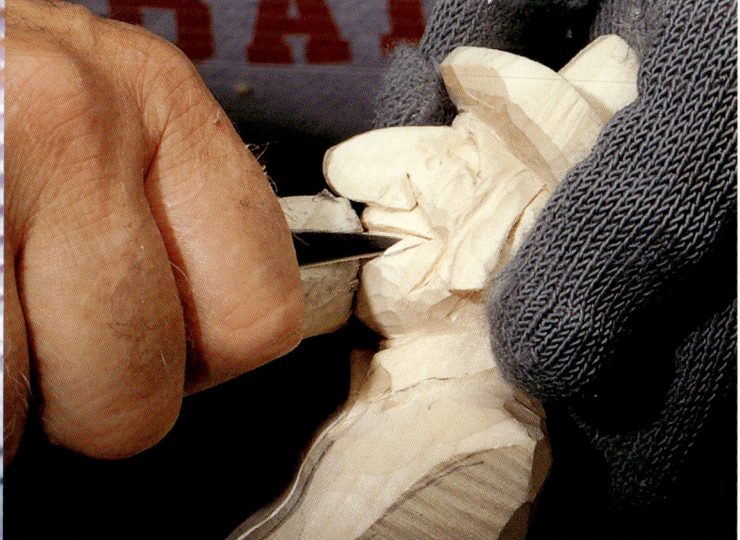

Cut along the lower lip line into the corner, take out the wedge. Repeat on the other corner.

Carvers often have trouble getting the lower lip and chin back as far as they should be. After I've drawn the teeth, I slice off the lower mouth and chin to guard against this tendency. Since this figure is exaggerated to the left the direction of the slice is this way.

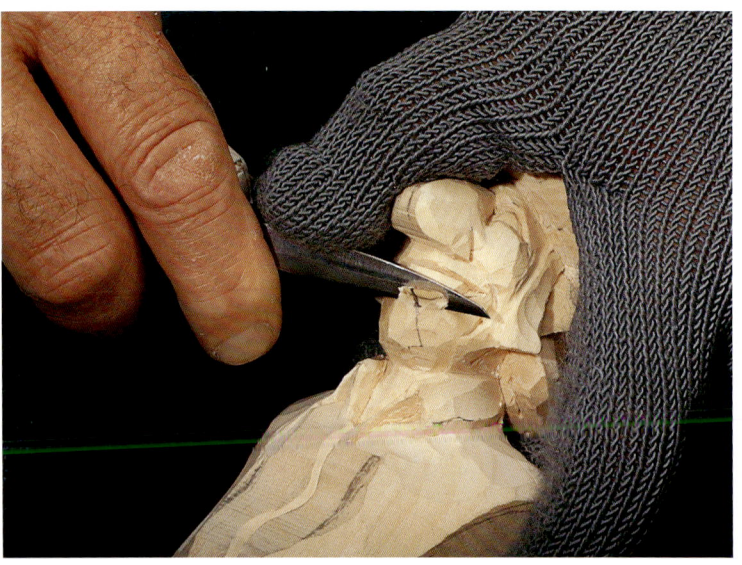

Working down from the tooth line, begin in the center and slice through the chin.

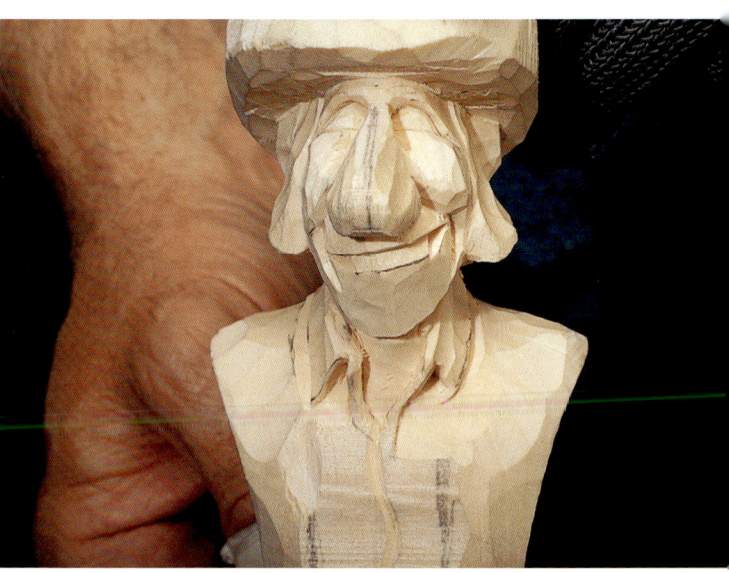

The result.

Move to one side and do the same thing.

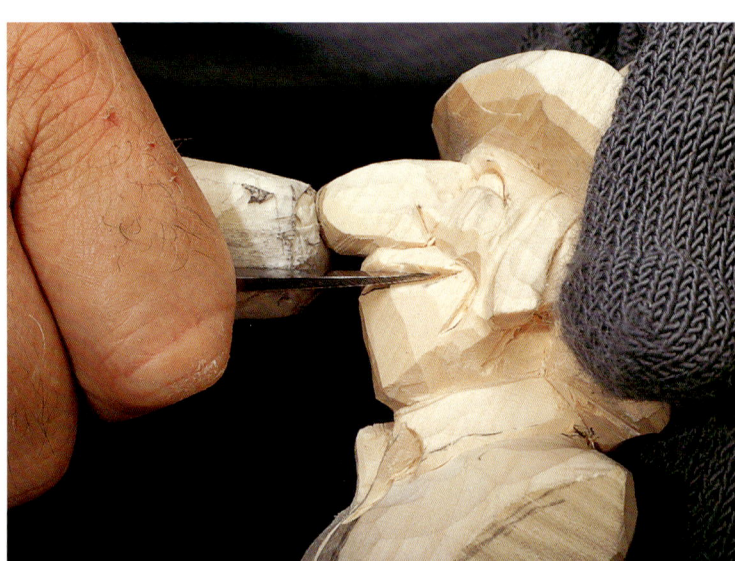

Blend the teeth area into the corners where the wedges were removed. You want a nice horseshoe shape to the tooth surface.

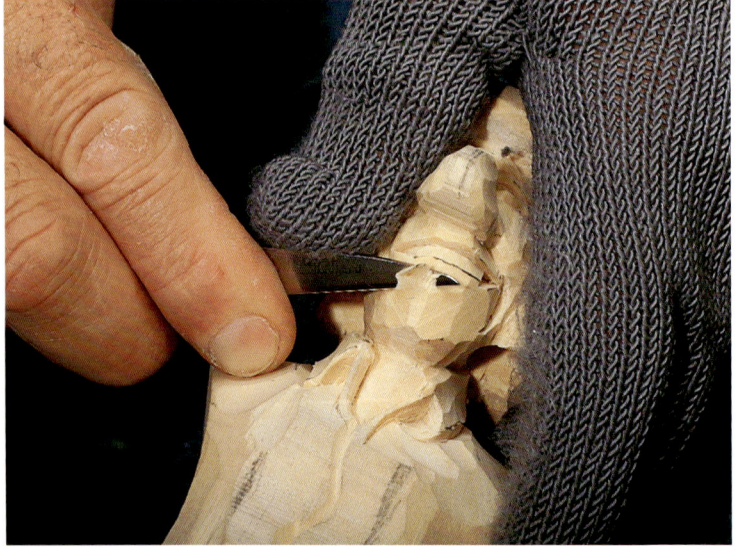

Then do the other side.

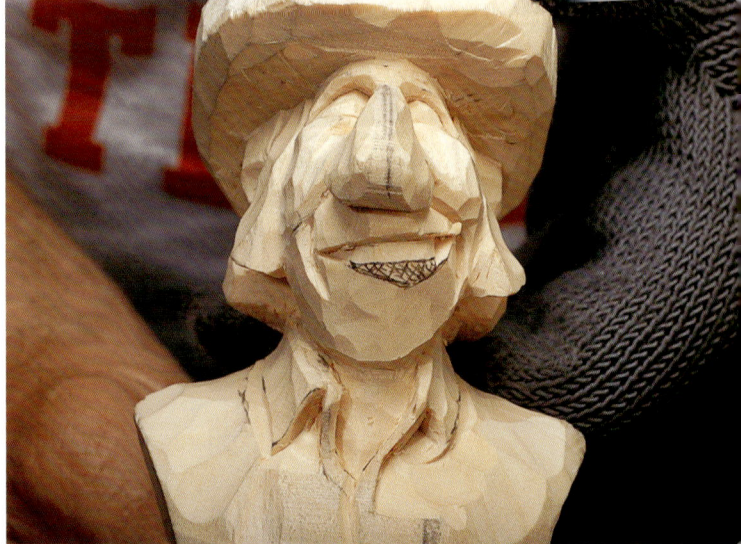

Redraw the bottom of the upper teeth and the top of the lower lip. The area between is marked for removal.

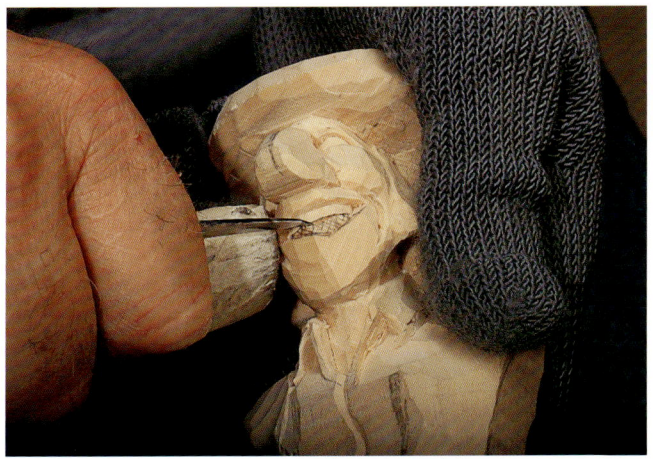

Make a stop cut along the bottom of the top teeth. This is cross grain, so I make several (sometimes as many as six) lighter cuts, instead of fewer heavier cuts.

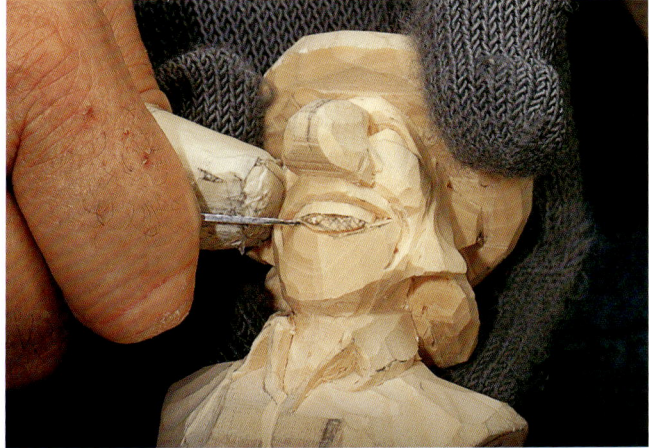

A wedge is cut by going along the top of the bottom lip at a slight angle. Again, don't try to do this is one cut. Several lighter cuts are preferable.

The result.

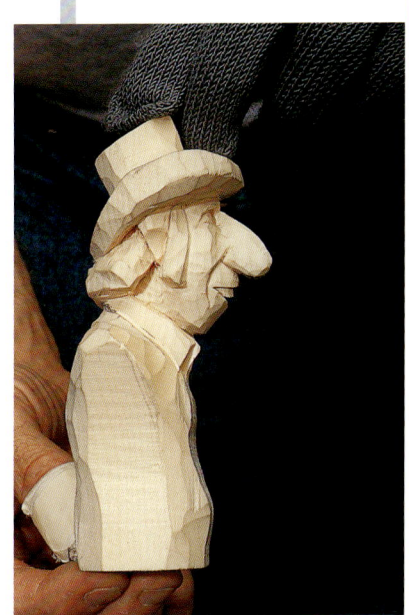

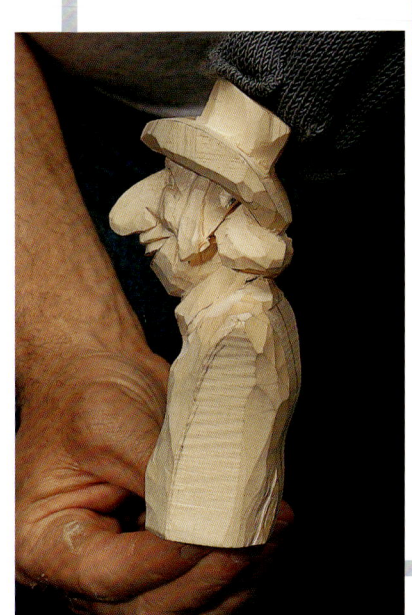

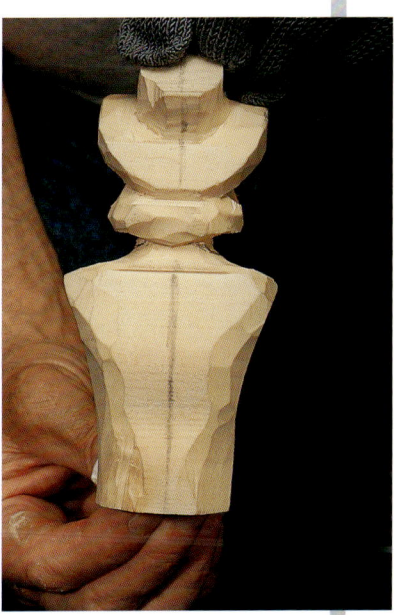

The figure is now ready for refinement.

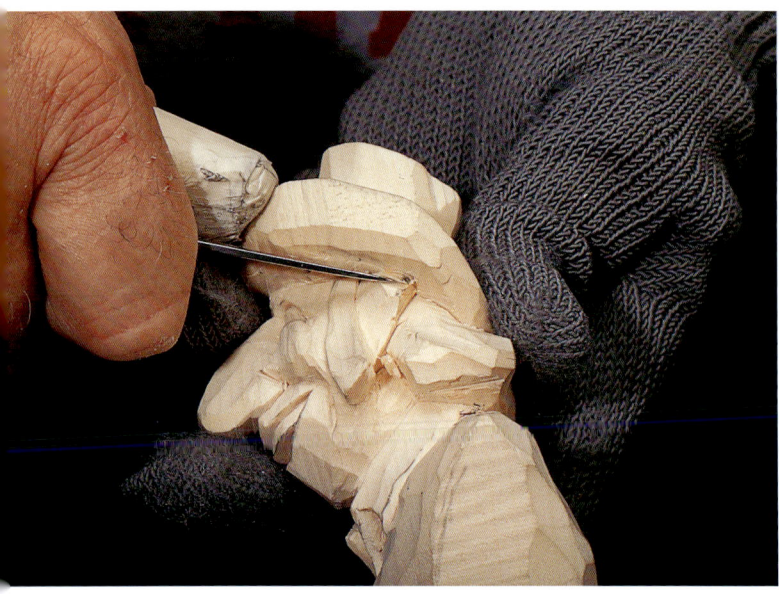

Cut a wedge at the top of the ears to give them some shape.

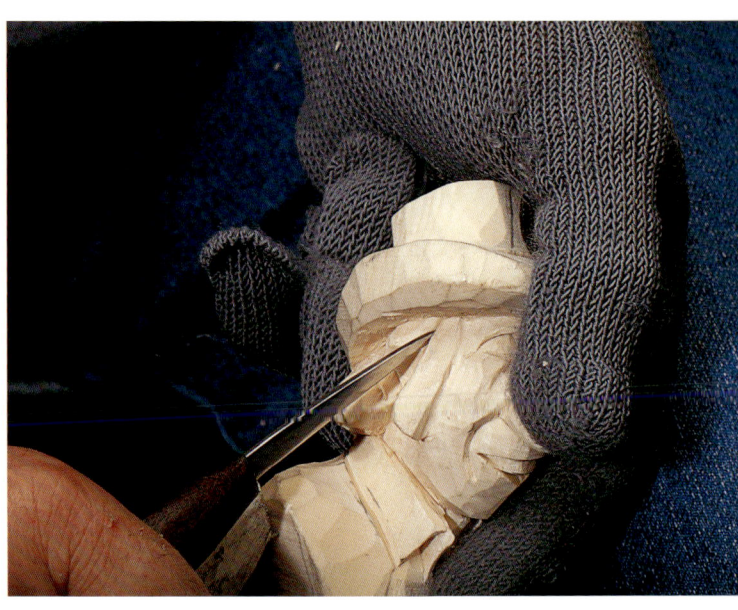

Make a stop cut behind the sideburn…

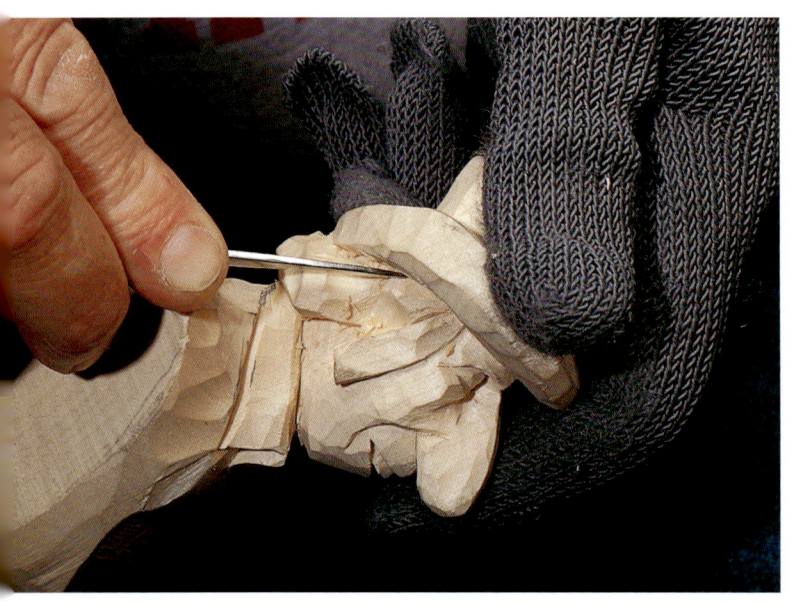

Take another wedge at the top back corner of the ear to give some curve.

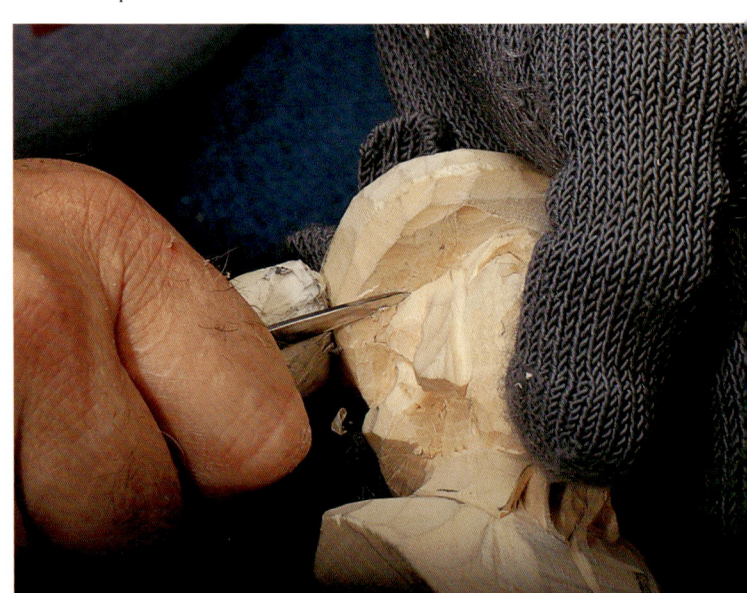

and under the brim.

The result.

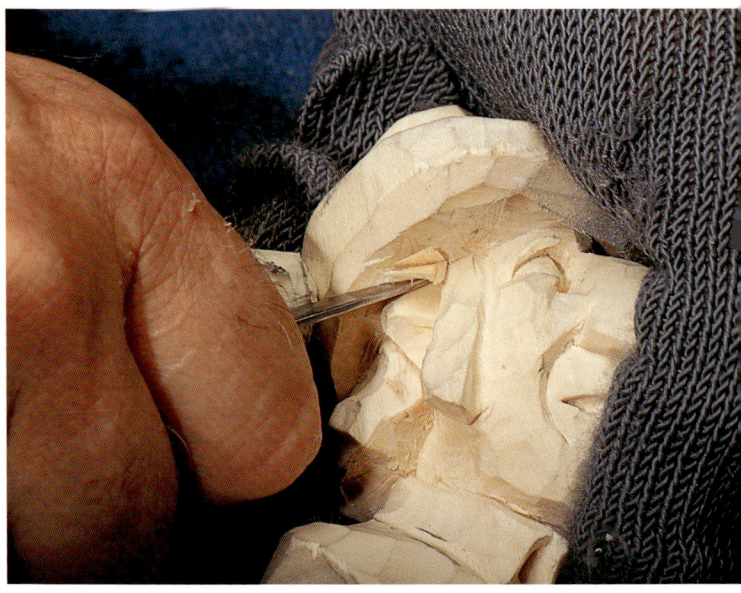

Cut a wedge along the surface of the ear back to the stop cut.

Soften any sharp edges in the ear.

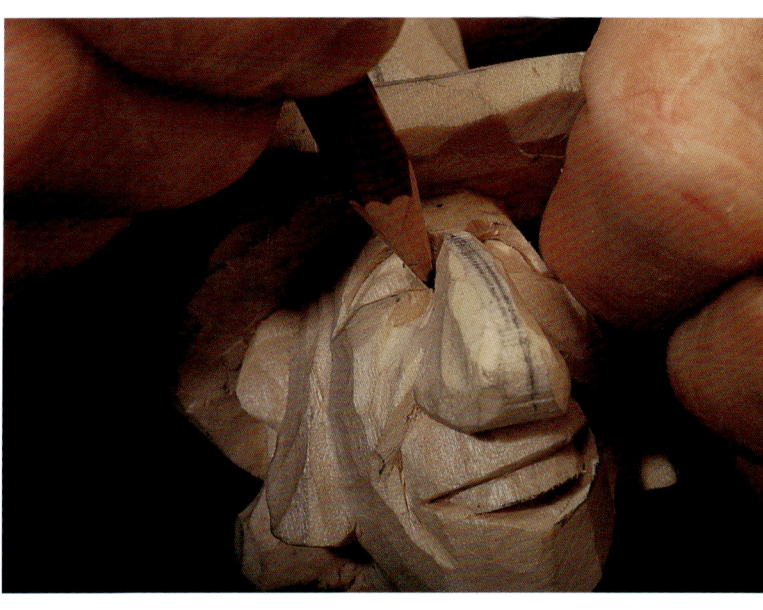

Start drawing the top eyelid at the corner next to the nose.

With a 3/8" Harmen #9 gouge I lightly scoop out the inside of the ear. I cut from just inside the outside edge back to the sideburn.

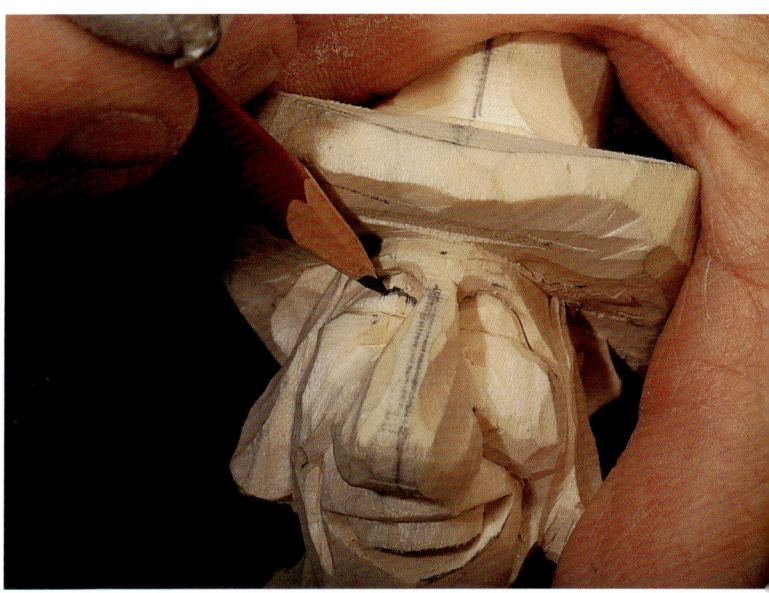

Continue around.

The result.

The result. Repeat on the other side.

Both eyes ready.

With the blade against the eyeball, pop out the corner between the lids. Repeat in the outside corner.

I make a shallow stop cut on the eyelids. Eyelids are not very thick. Make sure there is a sharp tip on the knife. At the corners I go deeper so I can use the line as a stop cut for the curvature of the eyeball. Most of this is cross grain so make a series of short shallow cuts.

Finally start at the top of the bottom eyelid and shave the surface of the eyeball so it looks like it goes under the eyelids, especially the upper lid.

Cut a stop in the line of the lower lid at the inside corner.

The result.

Draw in the teeth. I think fewer wider teeth are better than more small teeth. Since this is exaggerated I like to have the teeth slant slightly that way, even though in reality that doesn't happen.

Working back from the middle gap make a stop cut on the line between the two teeth…

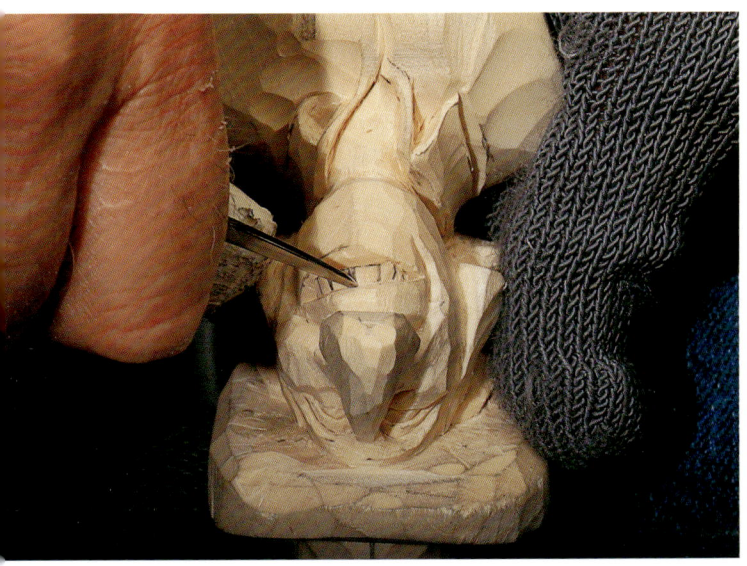

Make a stop cut at the top of the gap between the front teeth. I make it go up under the lip.

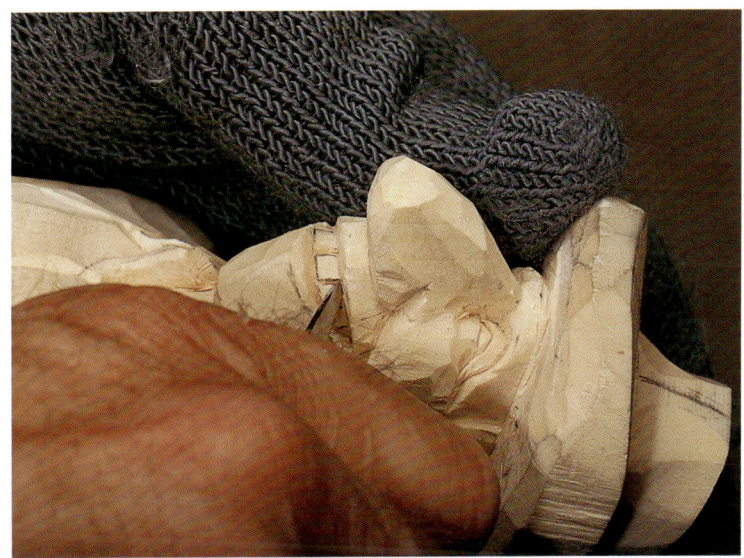

and a stop cut at the top of the tooth farthest back.

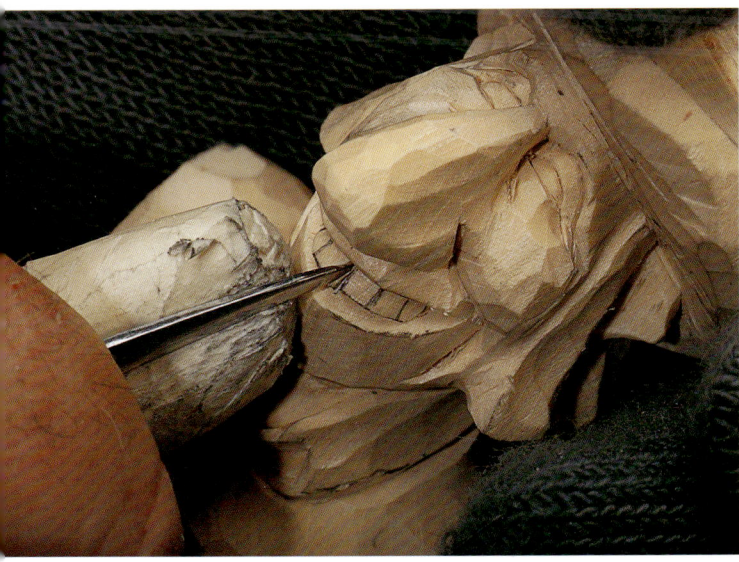

To create the gap I make a stop cut down the middle and cut a thin wedge from each side.

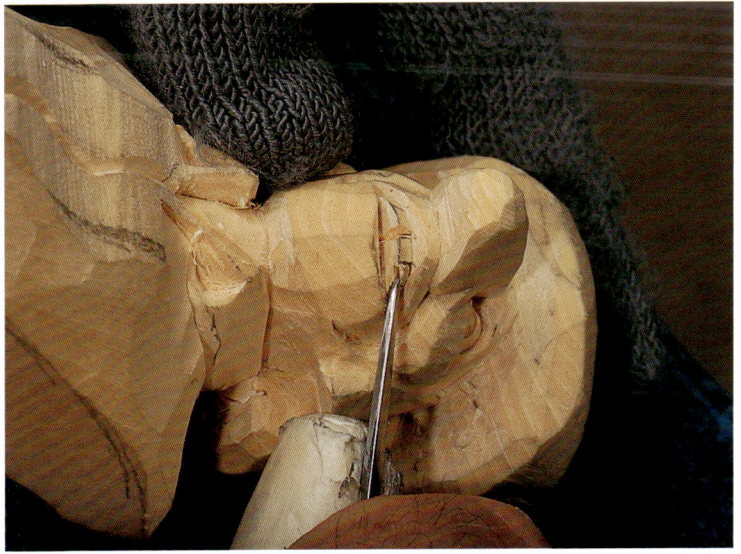

Cut a wedge on the back tooth only. This creates a stepped back effect.

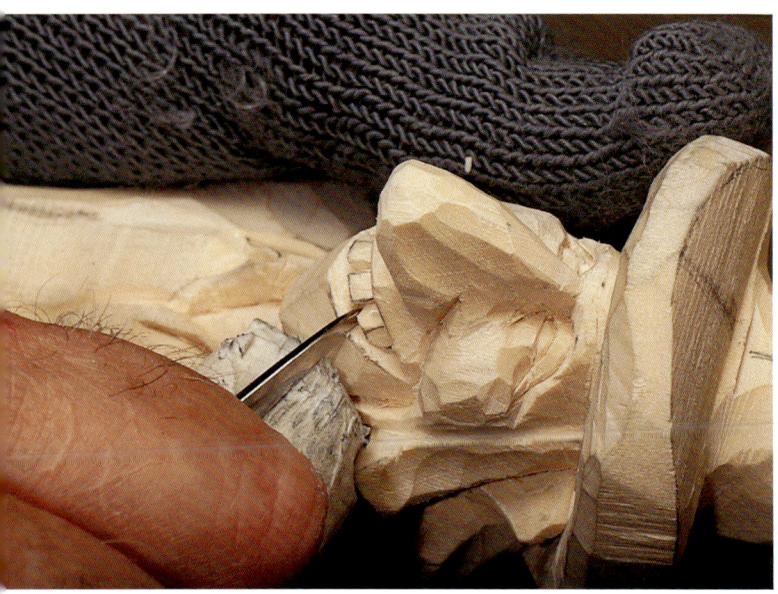

I also like to trim a bottom corner of the tooth to give an uneven look to the tooth line.

The teeth are finished.

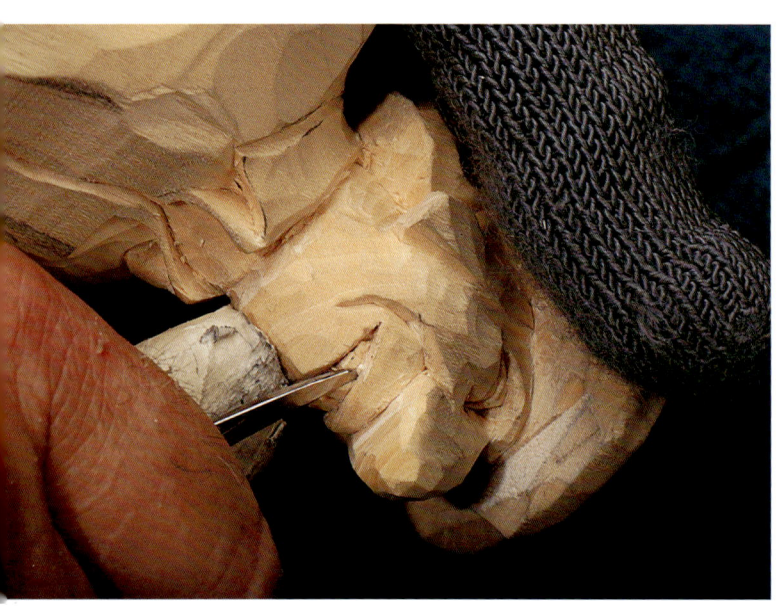

Finally I follow the contour of the teeth under the top lip creating a stop cut.

At the corners of the mouth a gouge makes the lower lip shorter than the upper, giving it a more natural appearance.

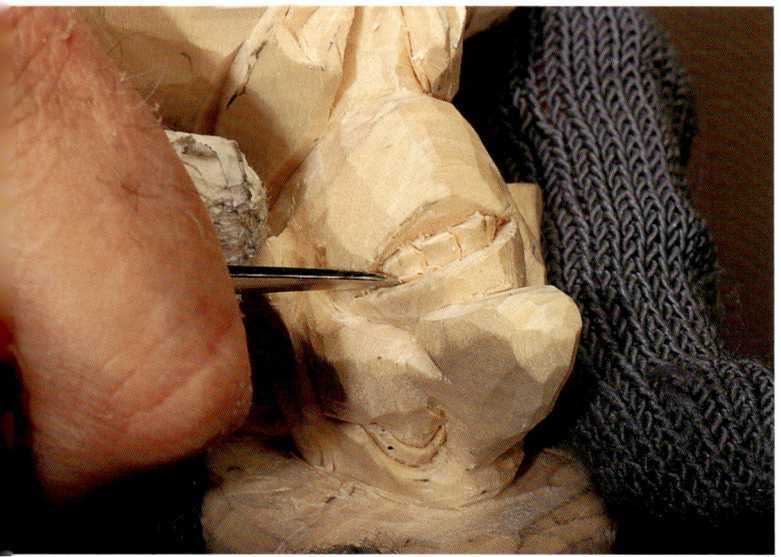

I then cut a wedge from the inside of the lip. This creates a nice shadow and makes it easier to paint.

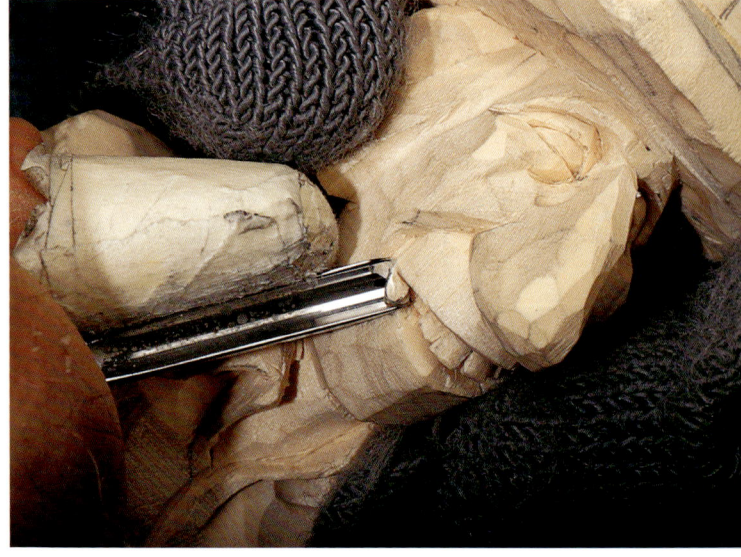

A Swiss #9/5mm gouge comes up at the corner...

for this result.

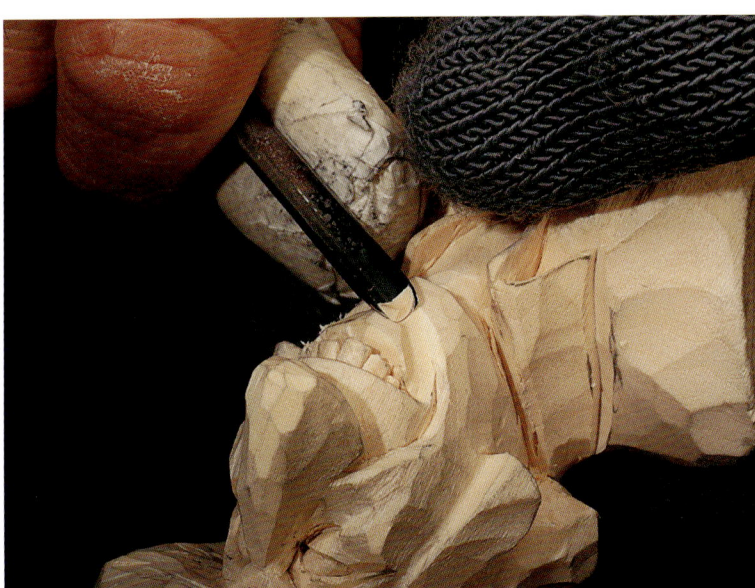

then connect the two.

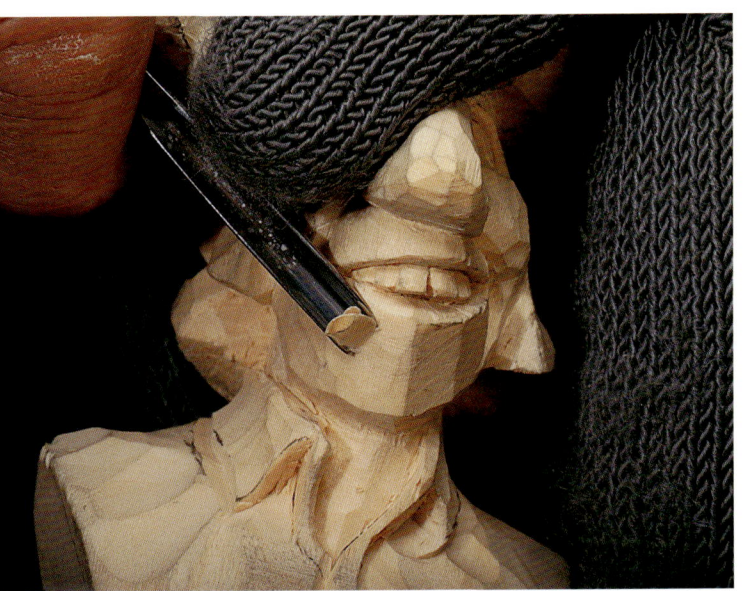

With the same gouge follow a line parallel to the lip, but slightly below it. This gives contour to the mandible. Come down one side…

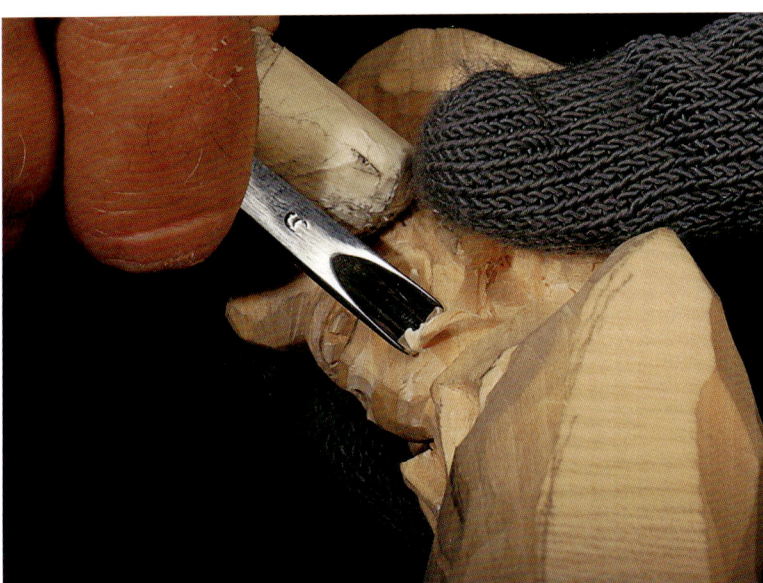

With a Harmen 3/8" #9 gouge come down from the smile line beside the chin on both sides. This will give shape to the chin.

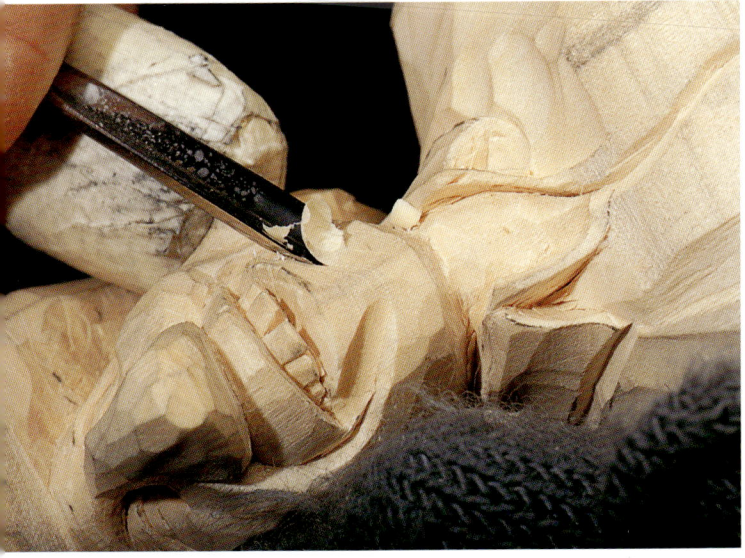

then the other…

Progress.

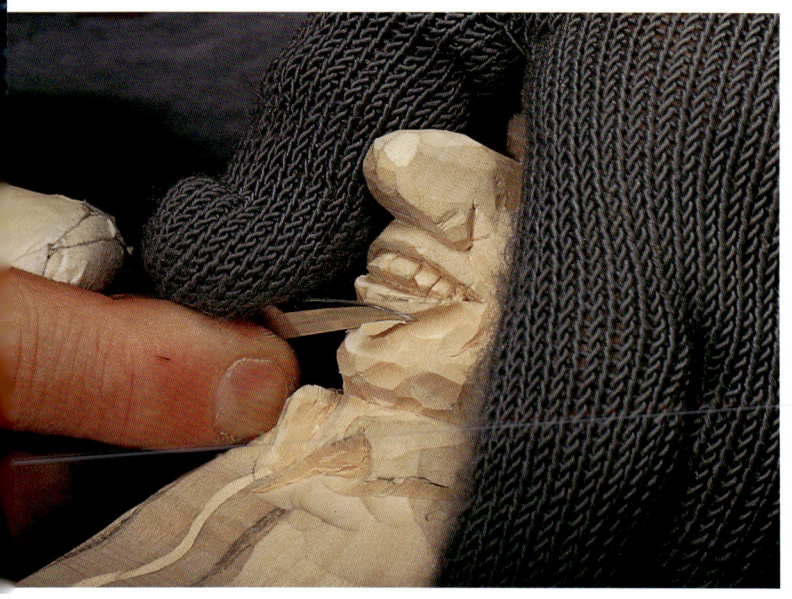

Go back and smooth sharp edges, blend the gouge marks, and generally clean the carving.

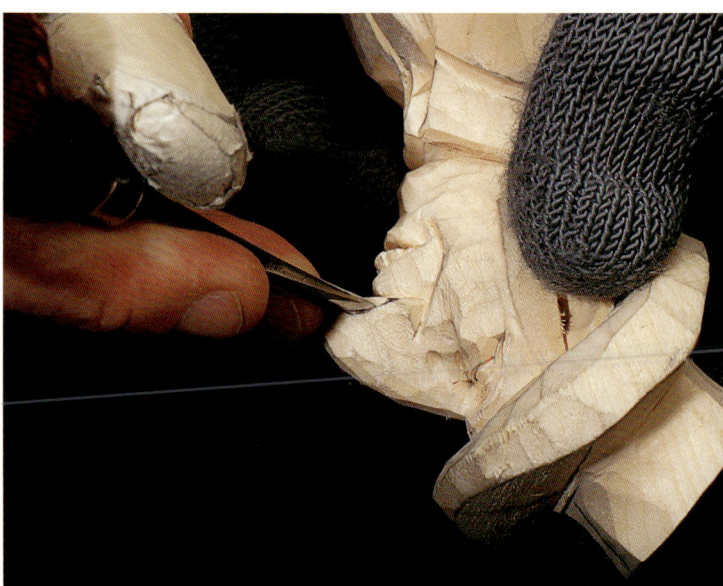

With the 3/8" #9 gouge come in at an angle and mark the front of the nostril.

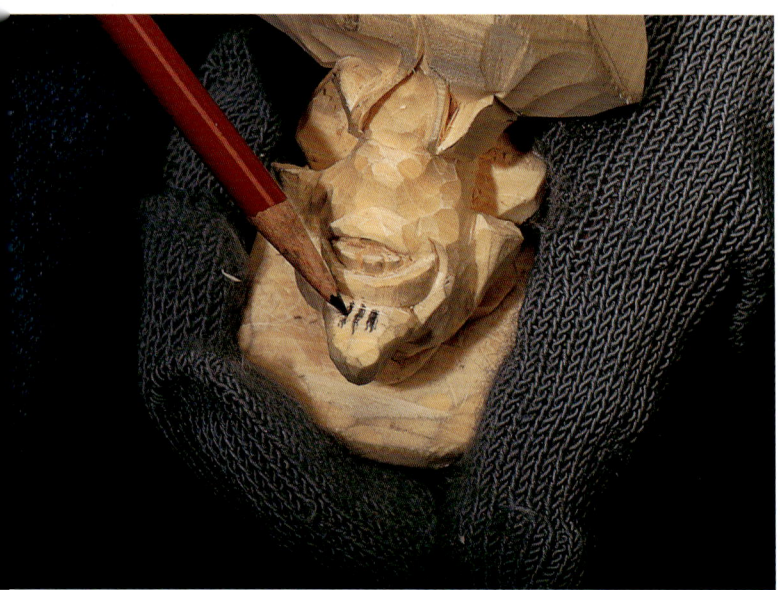

Under the noose draw a center line and two outside lines. The outside lines are the guides for the nostrils.

Turn the piece over and carry the nostril gouge back to the lip.

From there draw the nostrils.

The result.

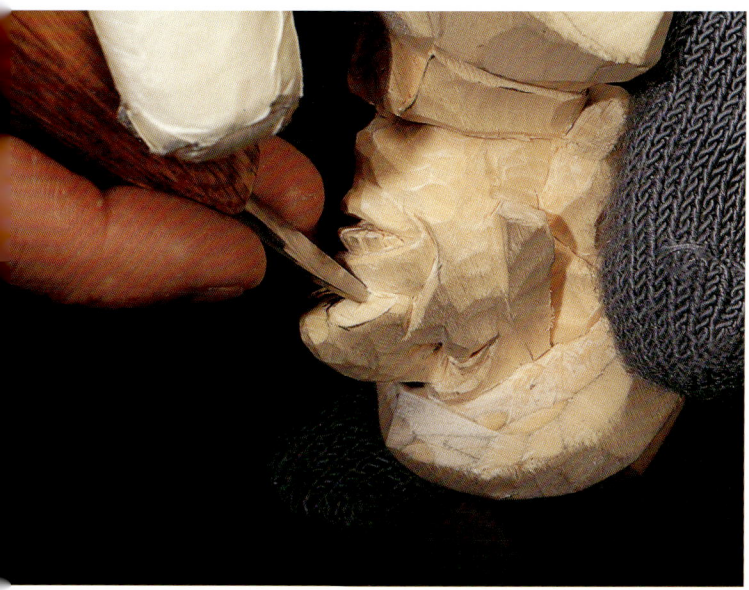

The nostril is deepened with a chip cut made by the knife. Make a cut parallel to the center mark…

The result.

one parallel to the outside…

The flange of the nostril is brought out with another chip carved wedge.

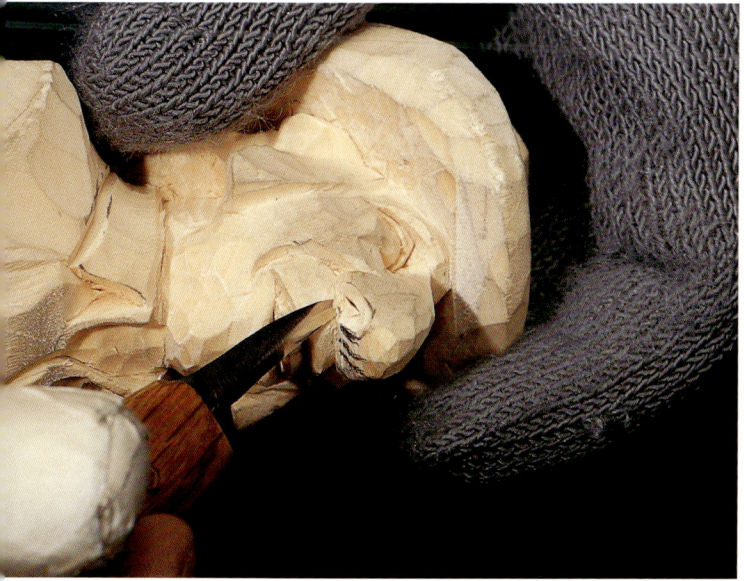

and take out the wedge with a cut at the back.

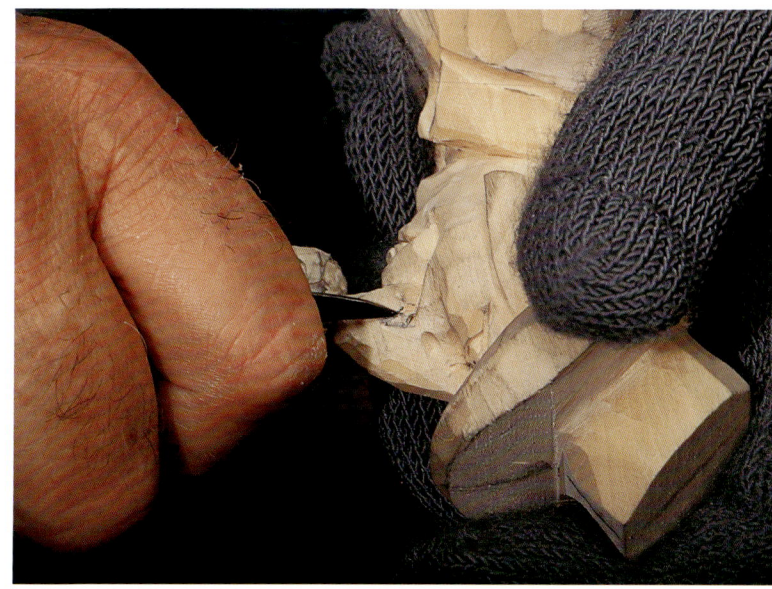

Make a stop cut along the nostril flare…

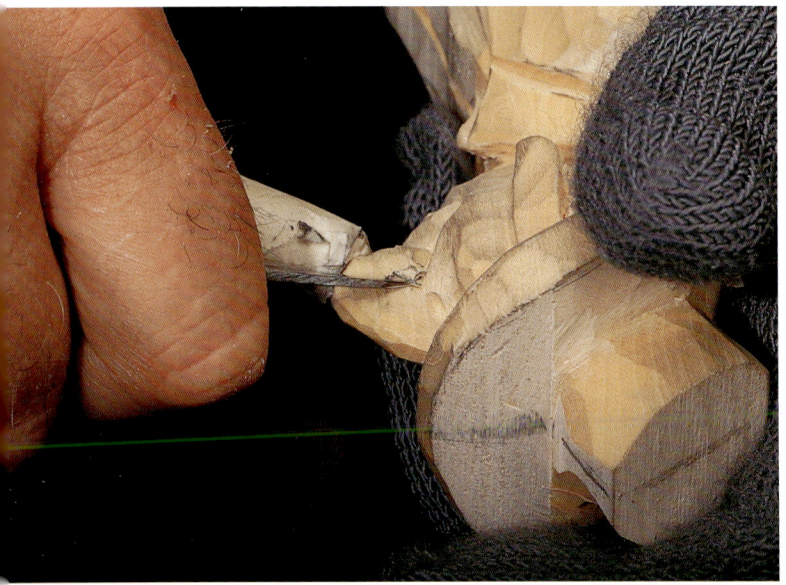

and trim back to it from above.

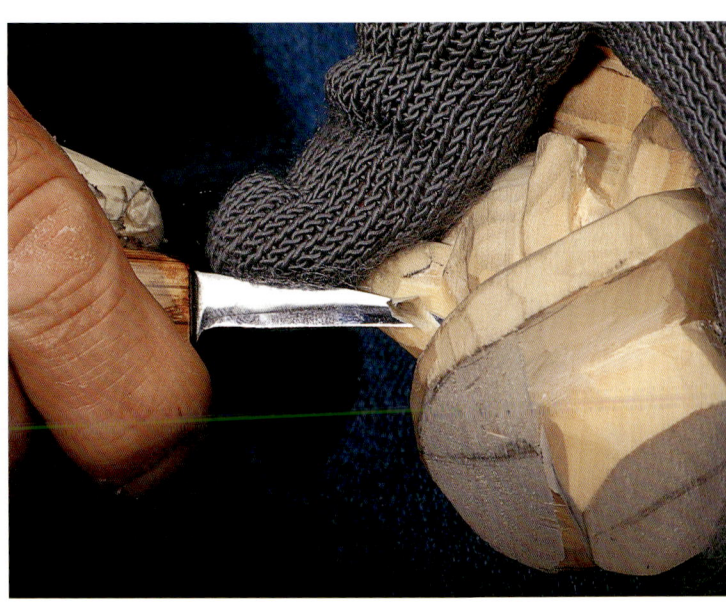

Blend the gouge mark with a knife. This thins the upper part of the nose to a more natural appearance.

The result.

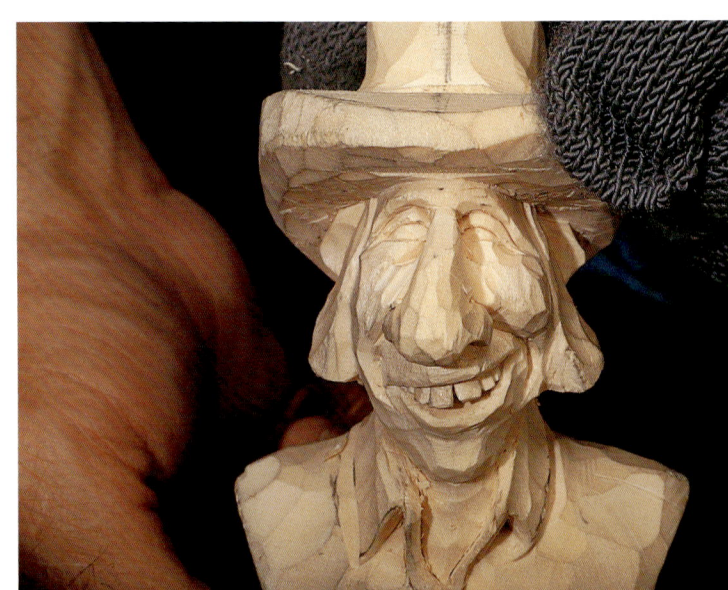

The result.

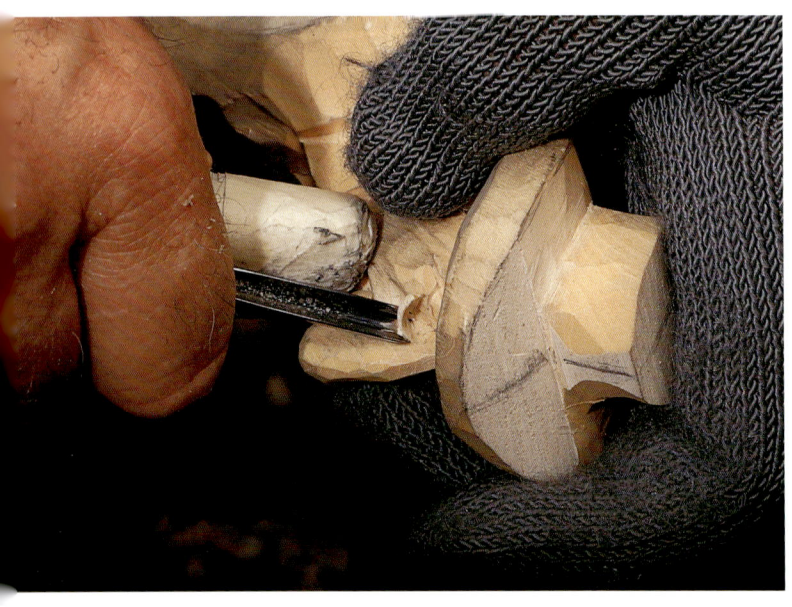

With Swiss #9/5mm gouge, start at the top of the chip just made and go up along side of the nose.

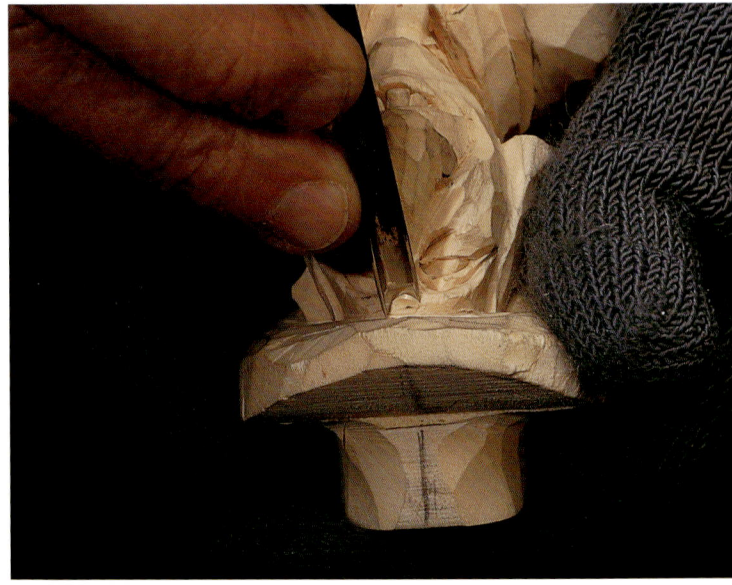

Gouge between the eyebrows to separate them.

I like to extend the nose a little higher by trimming back the eyebrow. Start by making a stop cut into the brow along side of the nose.

The result.

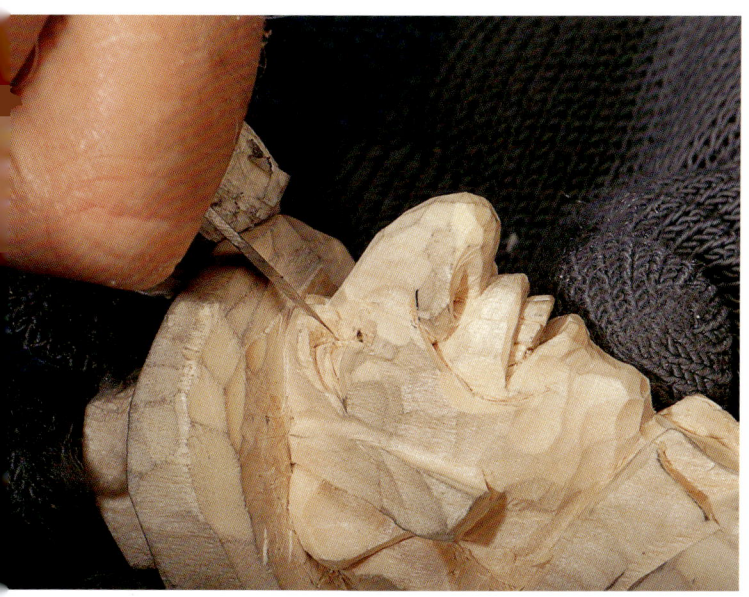

Cut back to it from the eyebrow.

Now we add contour to the face. Begin by drawing lines parallel and above expression lines.

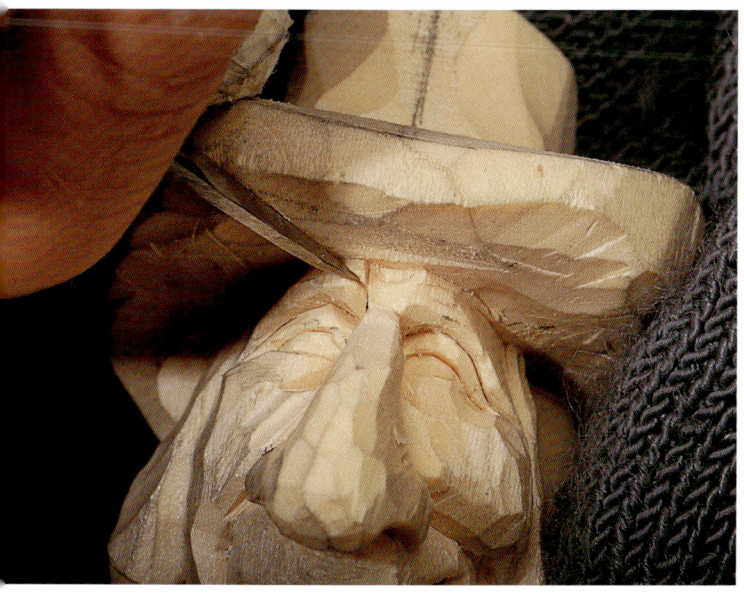

Finally trim the top corner of the eyebrow back to the brim of the hat. Repeat on the other side.

With a Swiss #9/5mm gouge follow the line. Because of the grain, work from the middle up and down.

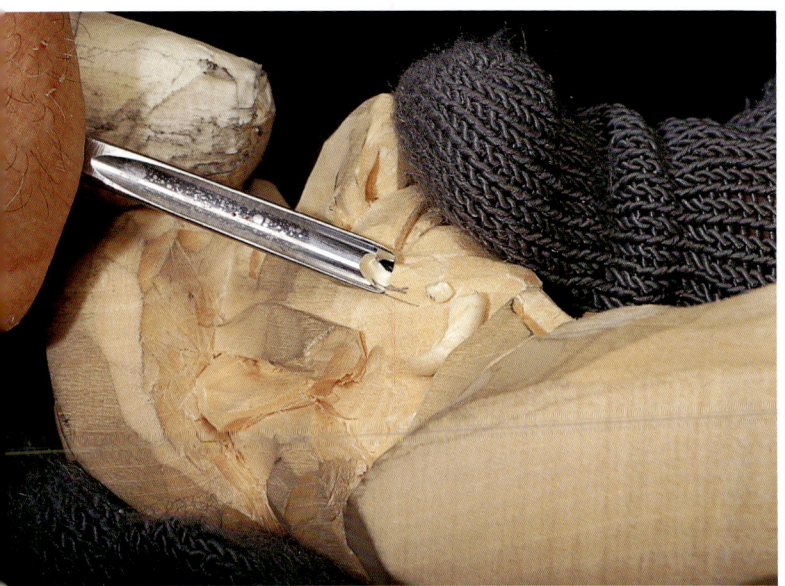

At the bottom end of the cut feather it out.

A second cut on the right is below the cheekbone about level with the earlobe.

One exaggerated left, the first cut is also in the temple but goes straight back.

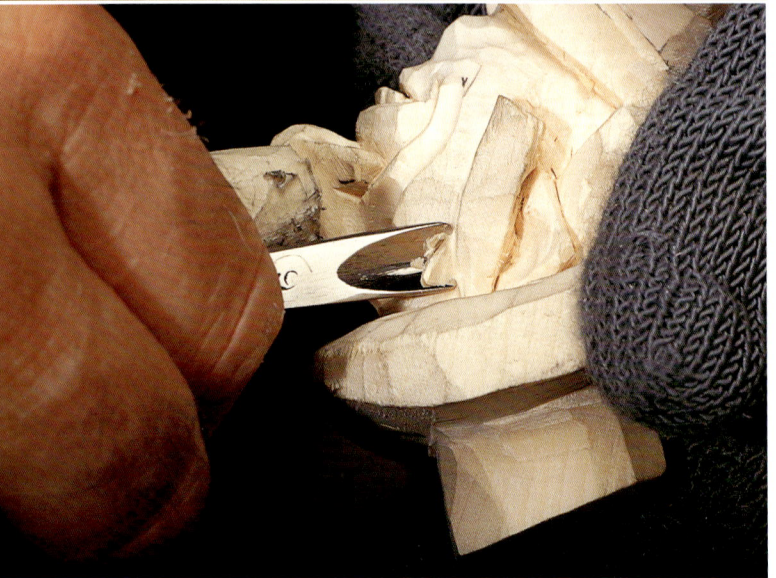

The contouring continues above and below the cheekbone with a 3/8" #9 Harmen gouge. This is an opportunity to bring out the exaggerated face even more. Starting on the left we go in on the temple at a slightly downward angle.

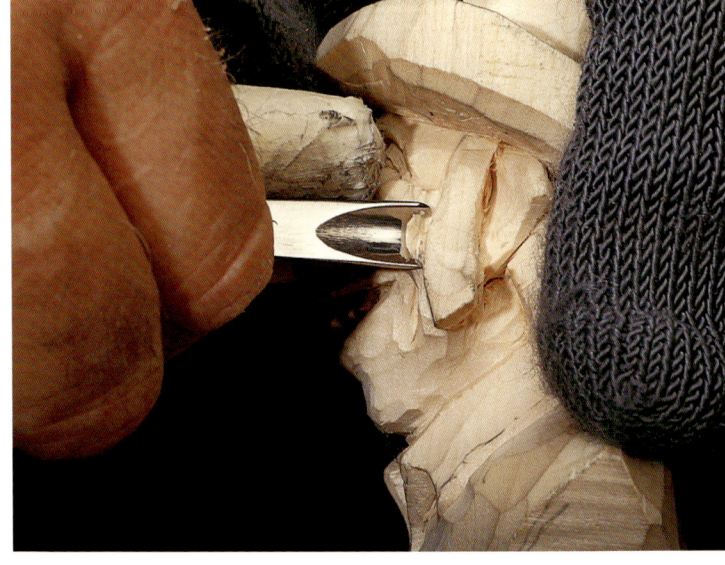

The second cut is below the cheekbone but higher than its mate on the right side.

The result. Those four gouge marks give the face all kinds of character and movement.

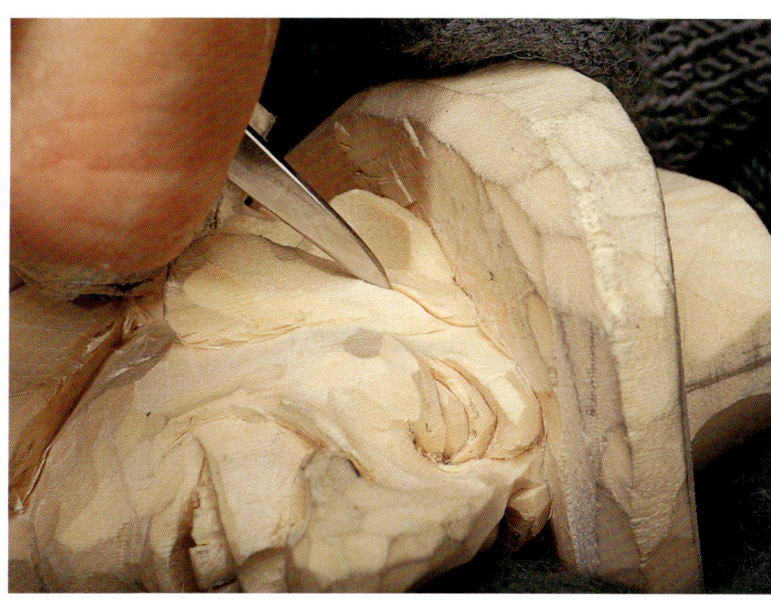

I want the hair to look like it is coming out from the head in a natural way. To do this I start at the top. Using a knife a cut a major stop line.

Clean-up and blend the gouge marks, getting rid of any sharp angles.

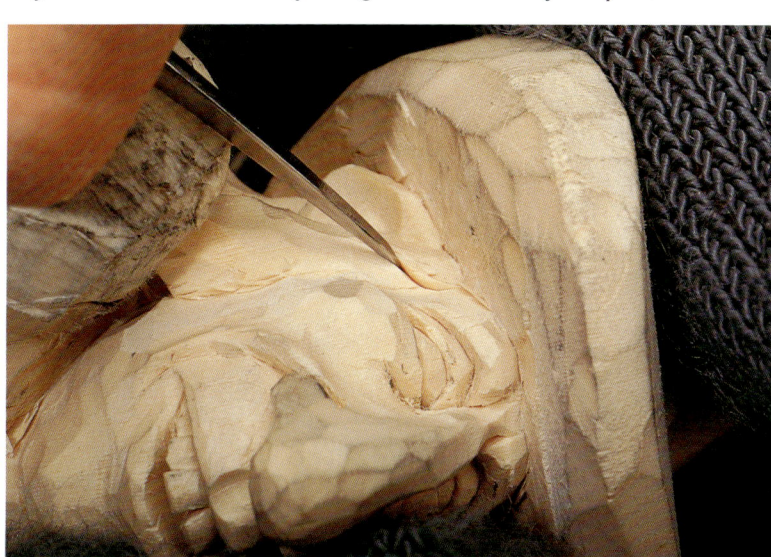

I then trim back to this from the face, cutting out a wedge.

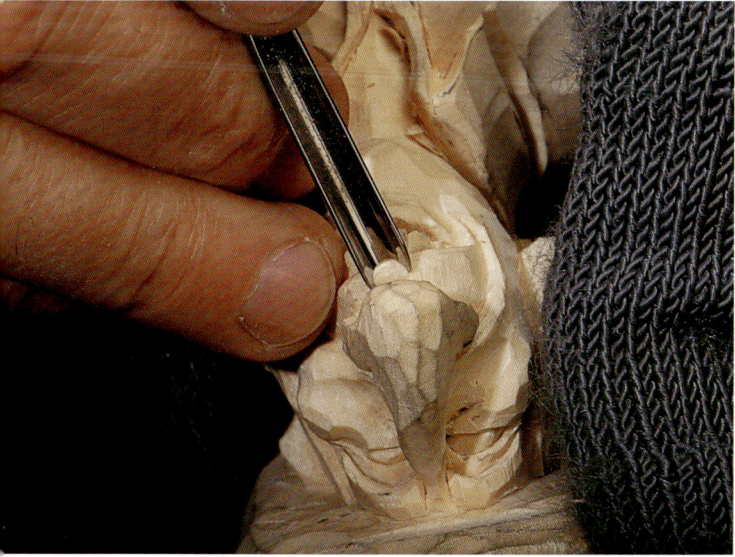

Use a gouge to add the philtrum. I try to follow the exaggeration of the face, giving it a little bend.

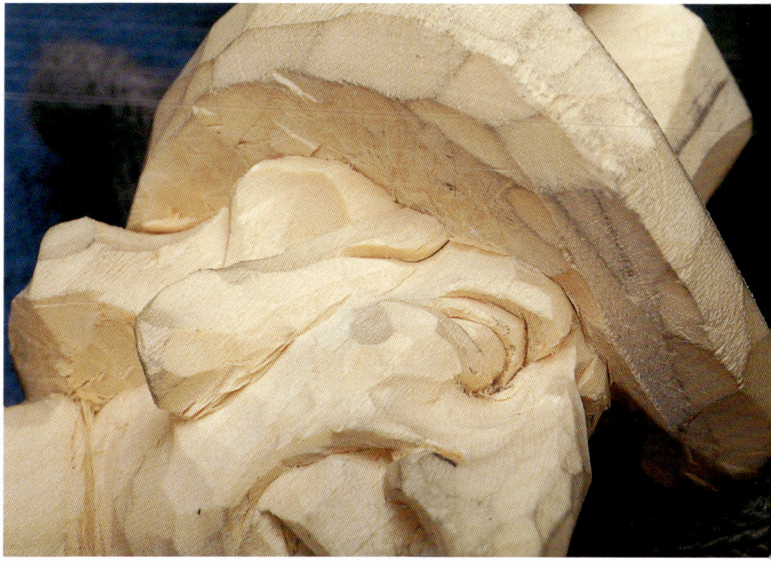

The result.

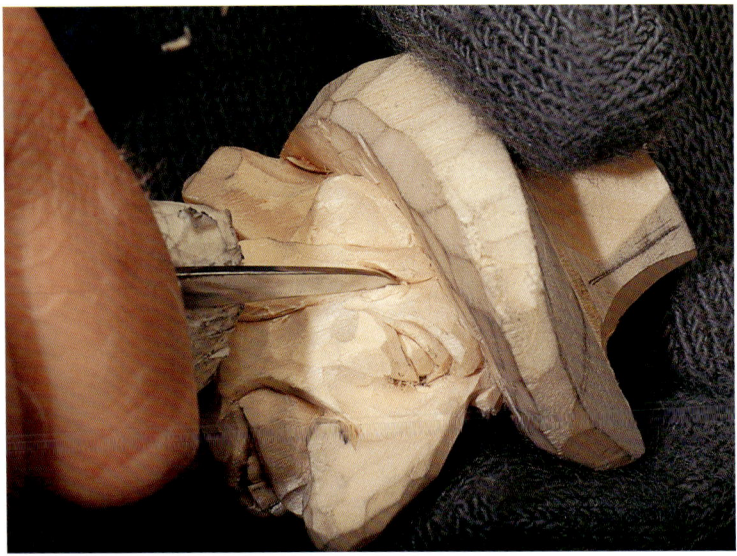

The second major line starts somewhere along the first, with the tip of the blade reaching under the first cut. This make it look as though the hair starts below the first.

With the three major strands defined I can fill in with more hair.

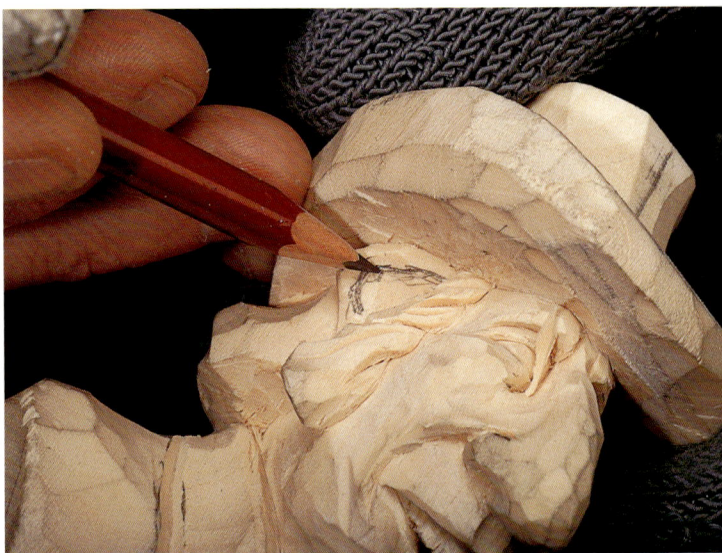

The same stop and trim technique is followed, though the hairs should each have their own shape.

I want the ears to look like they are being bent over by the hat. To do this I simply make a v-cut in the surface of the ear. This is the line.

The third strand begins under the second, and so forth.

At the top make a stop cut to about here.

50

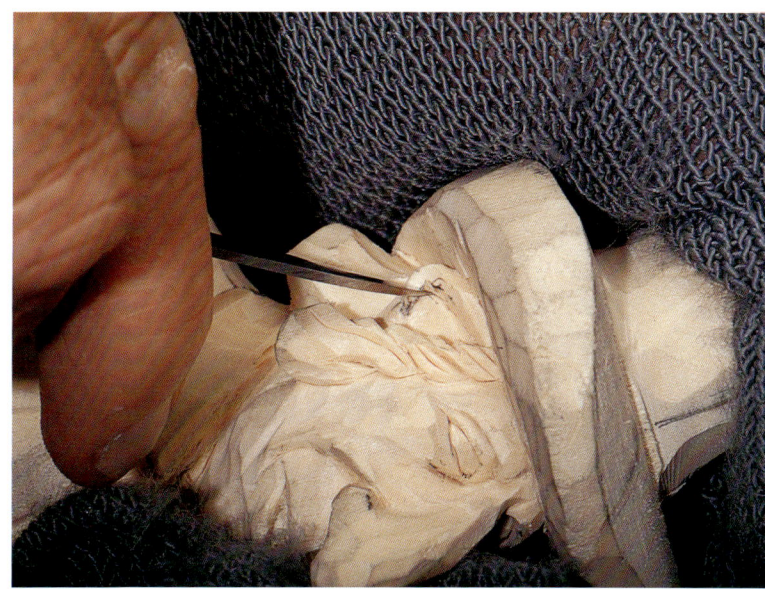

Cut wedges back to the stop cut to create shadow and depth.

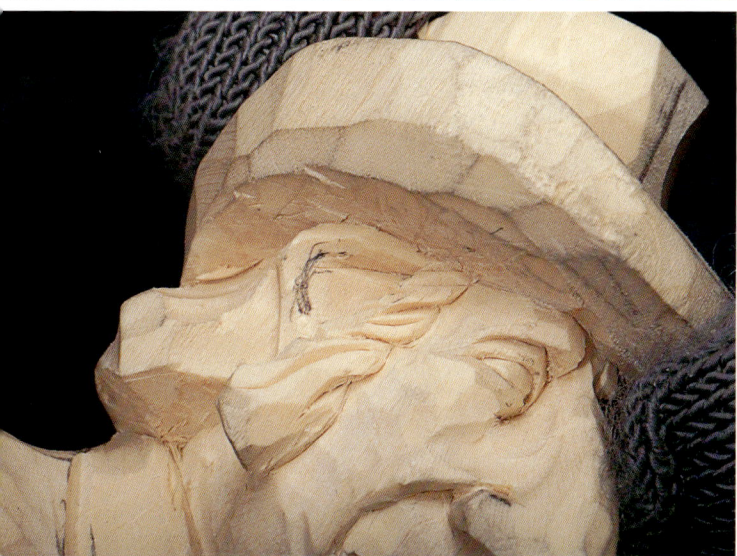

Trim back to it from the inside of the ear.

The result.

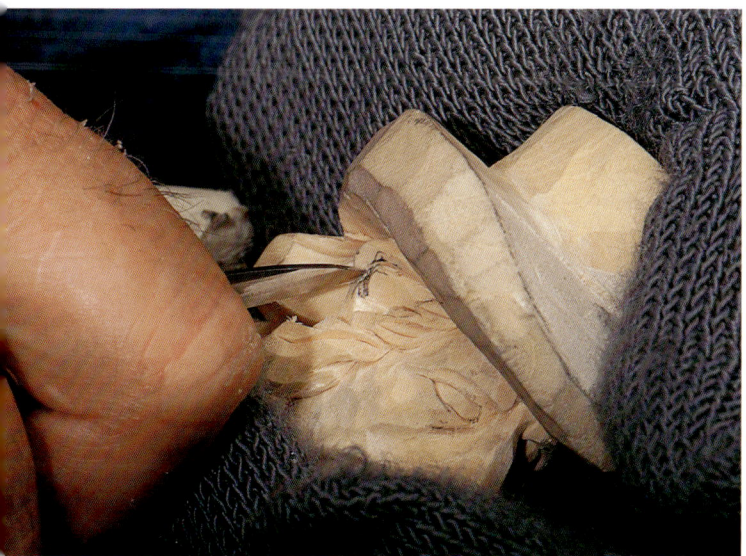

Continue with a deep cut on the rest of the line.

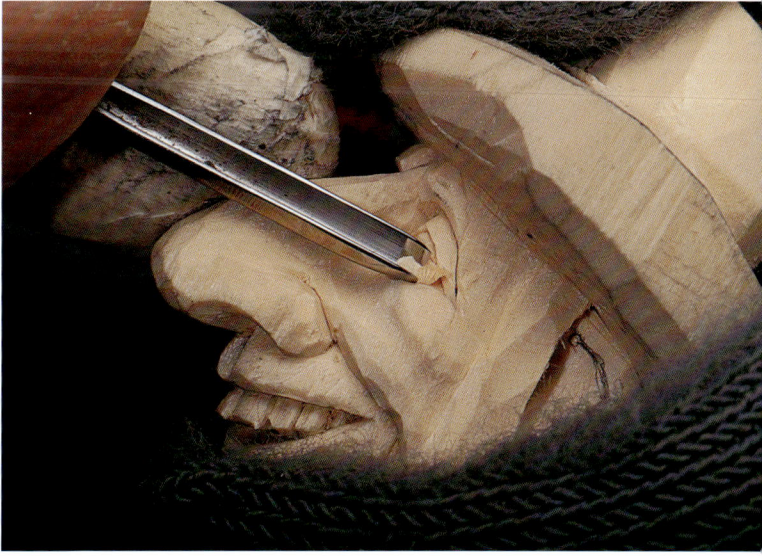

Eye sacks are added with a Swiss #11/3mm gouge. Start at the center and work out to the outside corner of the upper eyelid.

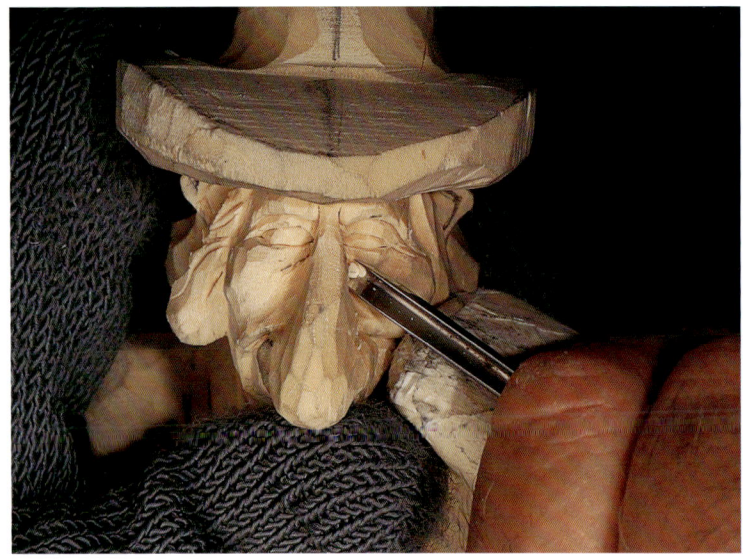

Start at the center again and work to the inside going as close as possible to the nose.

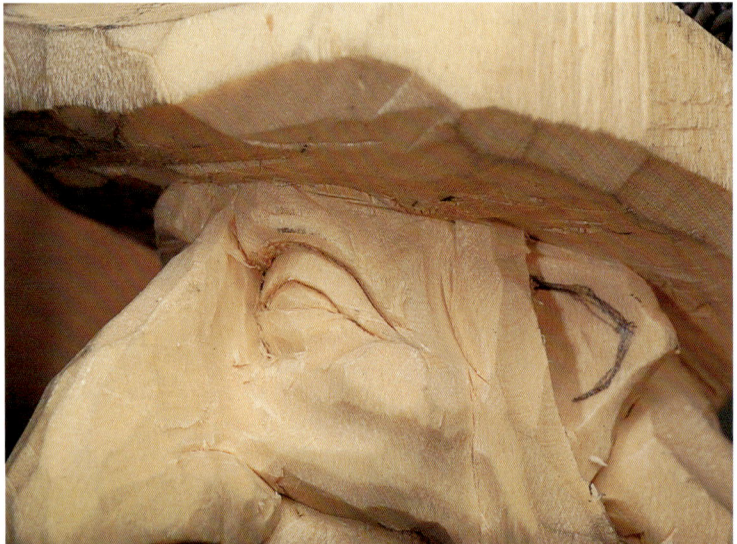

With a large flat gouge I carve around the joint of brim and crown. The hat has to look like it fits the head it sits on. So far this one is too big.

Continue to thin and shape the top side of the brim…

As you work, shape the crown as well. When the brim is thinner I start to give it a rounded effect.

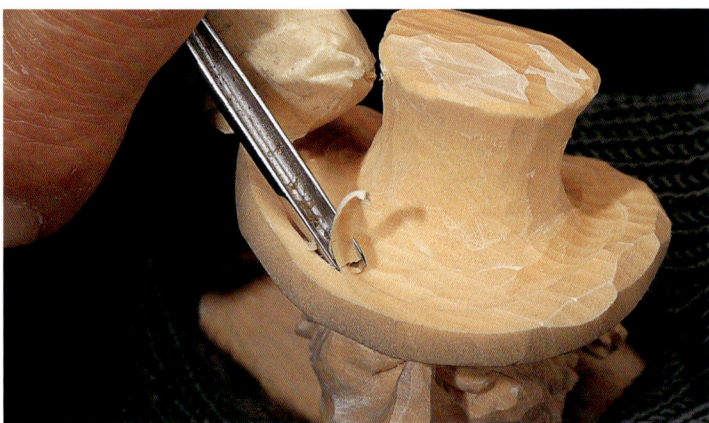

Run a Swiss #11/3mm gouge around the inside of the rim.

This creates the depth I need for rounding. Clean up the gouge cut, getting rid of the any ridges

Now with a knife I can round over the outside of the brim.

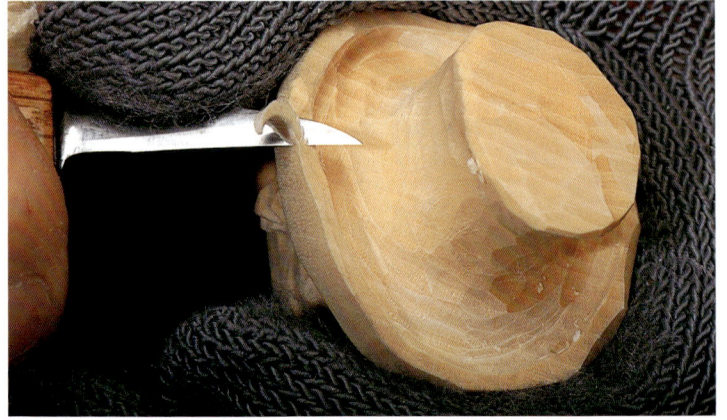

The finished brim

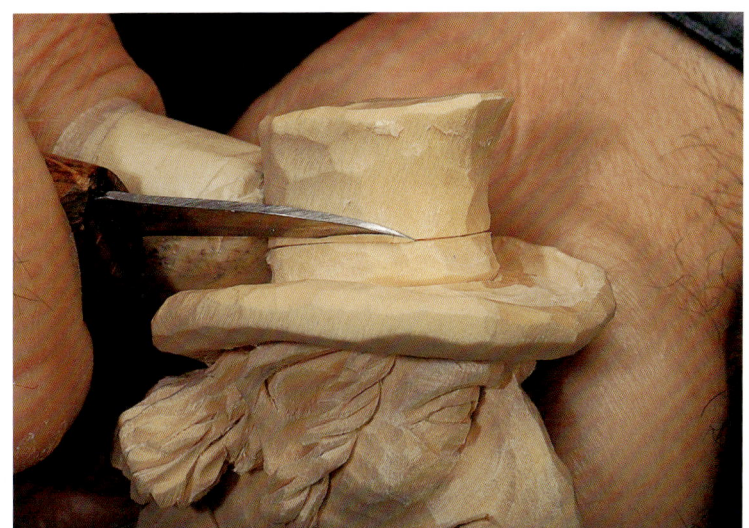

The top of the hatband is about 1/4" higher and is made in the same way. I cut straight in and slide the cut around parallel to the first line. This makes the stop cut.

Define the hatband. I use a knife, but you could use a v-tool. Make a stop cut where the crown meets the brim.

Cut back to the stop from above, taking out a wedge.

Cut back to it from the crown, taking out a wedge.

Clean up the carving for this result.

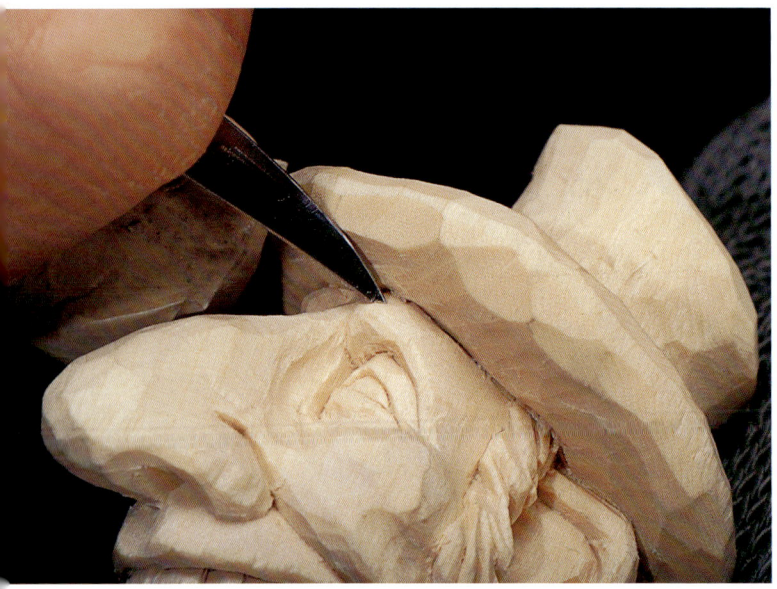

The eyebrows are created with a series of wedge cuts made with the tip of the knife.

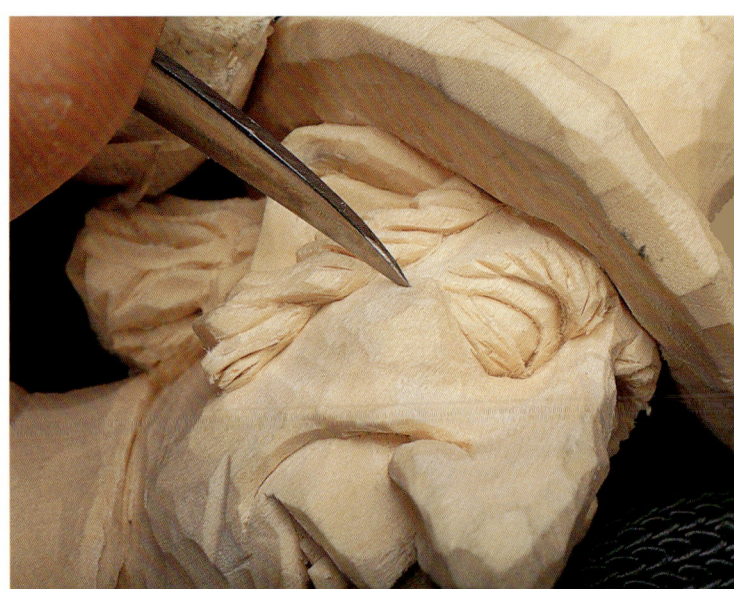

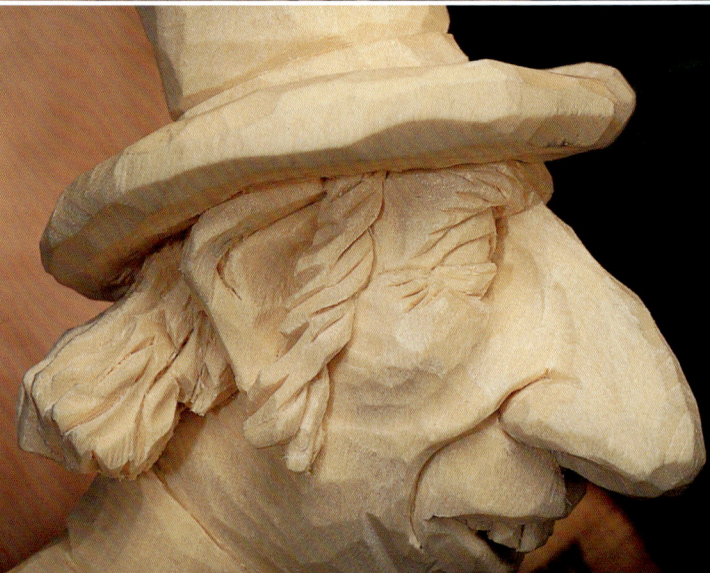

Use the tip of the knife to take small wedges out at the outside corners of the eyes for crow's feet.

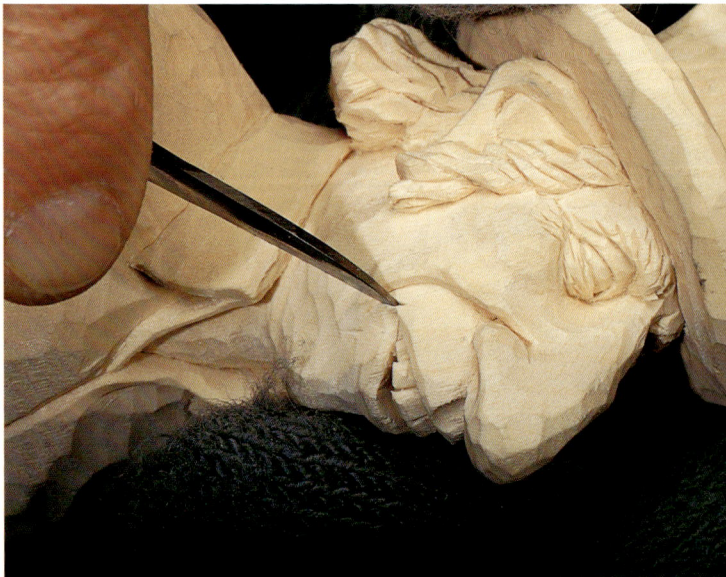

Add some wrinkles on the sacks under the eyes. This will give shadow detail to the face. The cut is a small wedge taken with the knife.

I make a triangular chip cut at the outer corners of the mouth to create shadow. The first cut down at the outside corner.

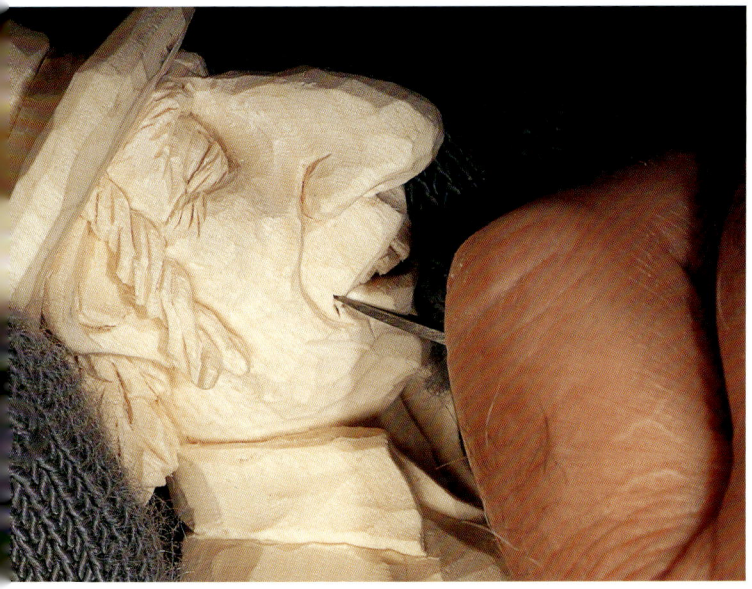

to second is along the upper lip

Now we move to the finishing touches of the body. Lower the right side of the chest using a gouge. This is the side that is buttoned under.

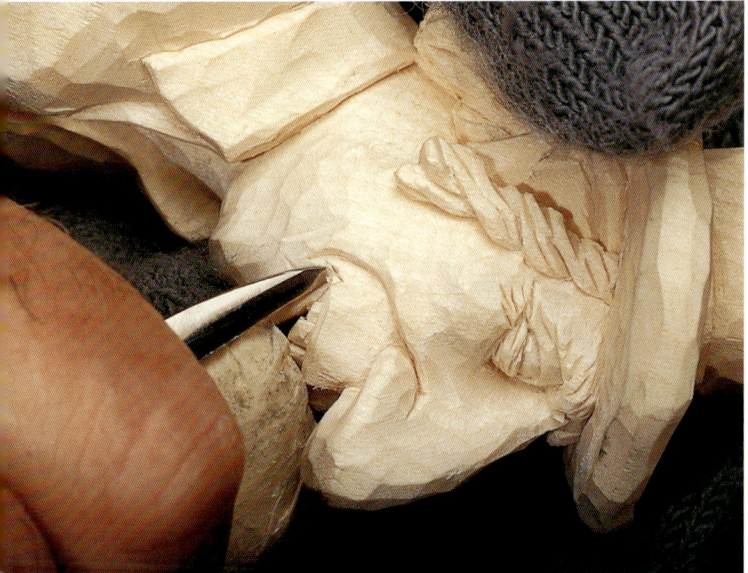

The third is on the lower lip and pops out the chip.

Mark the positions of the buttons.

The resulting dimple.

Scoop out the button area with a Swiss #9/10mm gouge.

Draw in the buttons.

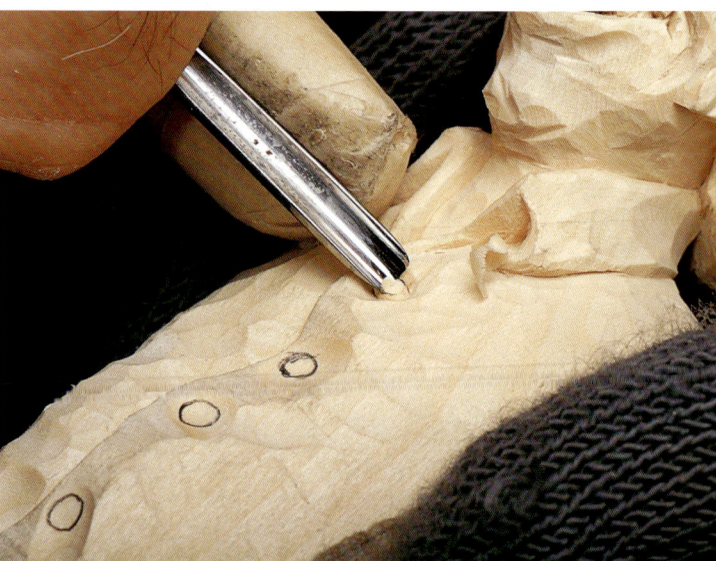

Next I use the same gouge to go across the grain on the surface of the button to make it slightly concave.

Make a stop cut around the button straight in or slightly beveled outwards.

When the buttons are set, clean up the left side of the chest, giving a little motion to the clothing as you carve.

Come back to the button from all around with a Swiss #9/5mm gouge.

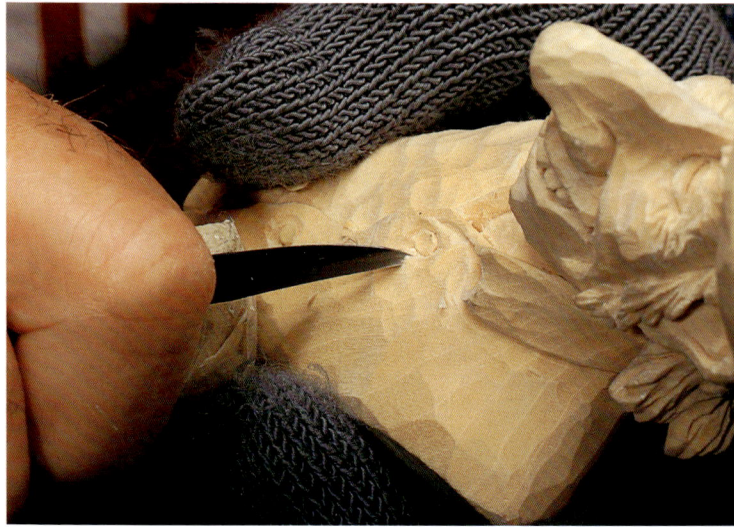

The cloth around the buttons needs some stretch marks. These are added randomly, two around one button, three around another. Some long, some short. They are made by cutting wedges with the knife.

To create a shadow at the shirt opening I cut a sliding wedge. The first cut follows the opening and is fairly flat, going under the flap.

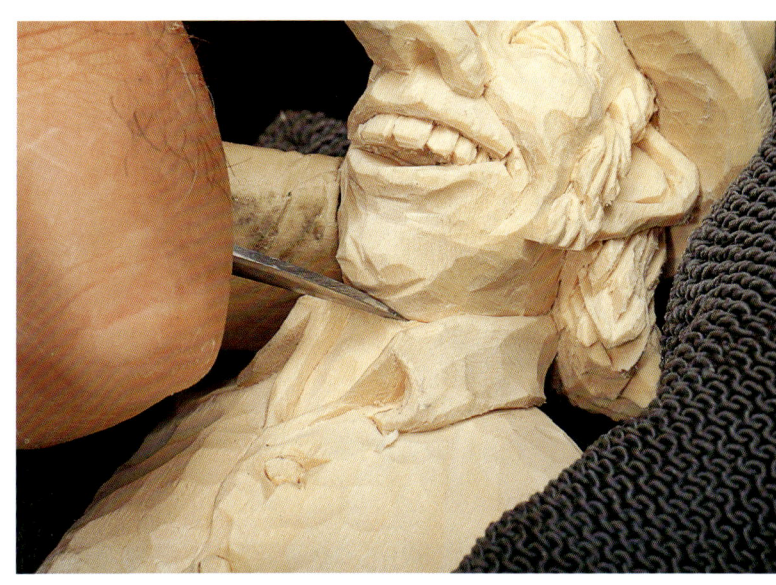

To create a tee-shirt, make a stop cut at the neck opening…

The second cut is even flatter, cutting a wedge as it slides down the shirt opening.

and trim back to it from the neck.

Use the same technique under the collar to separate it from the shirt.

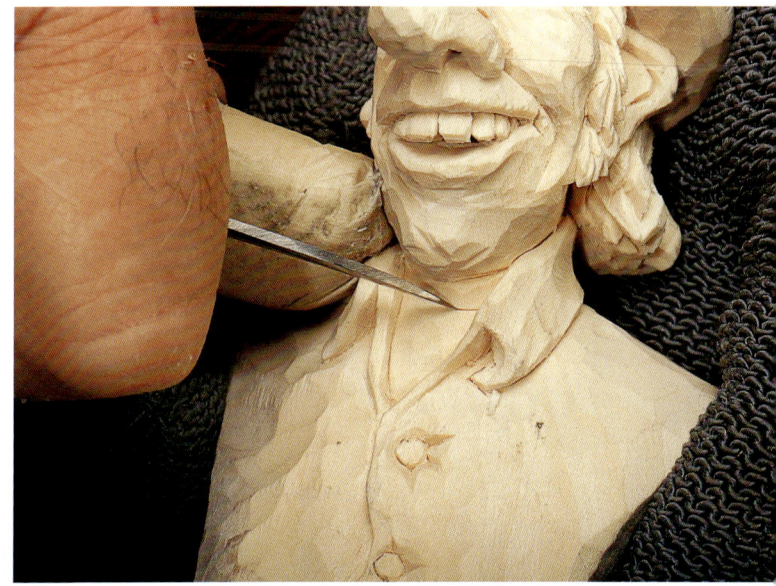

The tee-shirt collar band is created with another stop cut a little lower, with a sliding wedge cut back to it.

57

Progress.

Create two buttons on the open vest as you did on the shirt. Locate their position, gouge the space, cut the buttons, and contour the buttons. Because there is nothing pulling on them, I do not add the stress lines.

Draw in the lines of the vest. On the right side I want it flared out a little.

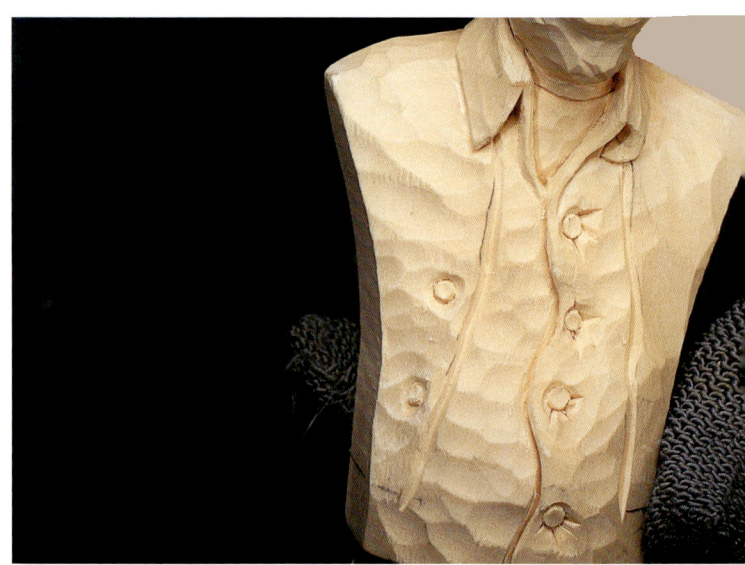

The result.

Follow the vest line with a v-tool.

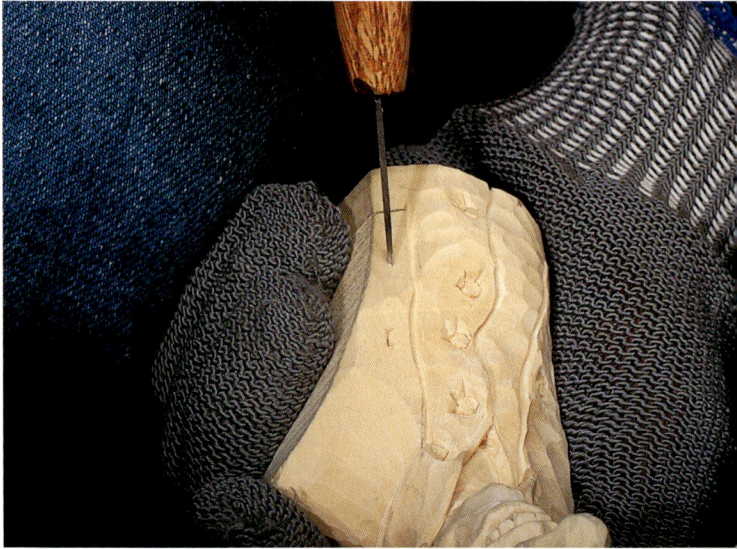

Across from each button we need a buttonhole. These are made by making a vertical stab cut.

This is followed by another stab cut at the top…

then the other.

and one at the bottom.

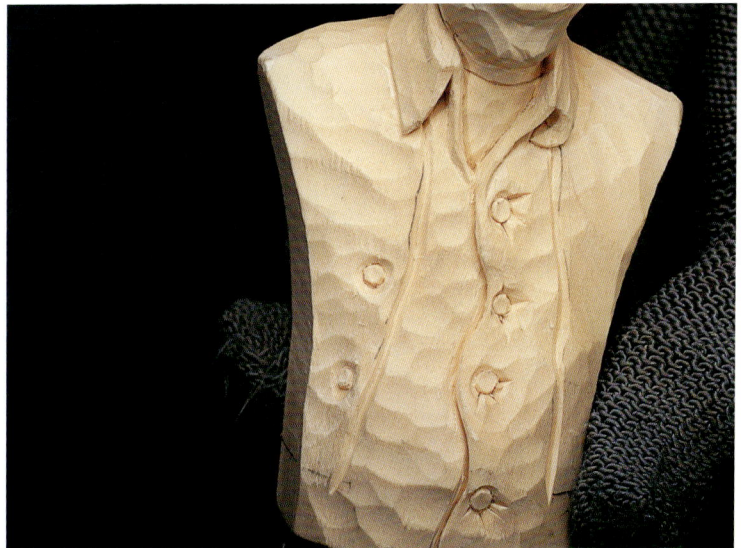

The result.

The hole is finished by taking to triangular wedges out at the top and the bottom of the vertical cut. First go to one side…

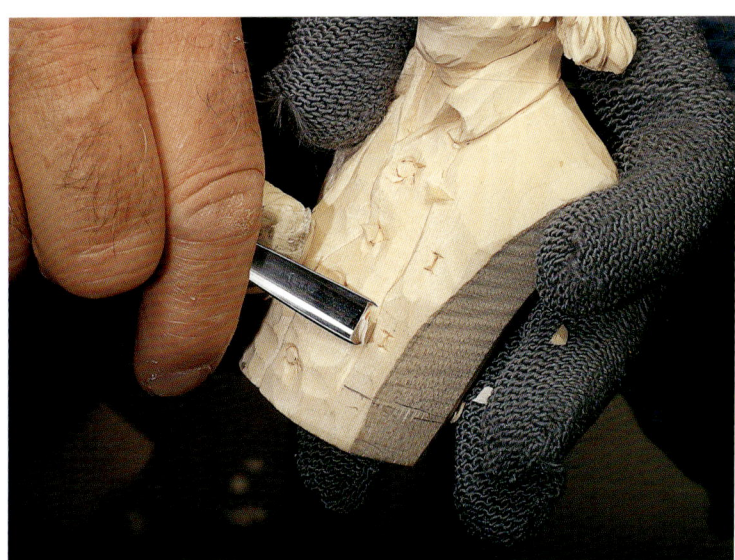

Reduce the shirt so it appears to go under the vest.

Undercut the edges of the vest with a sliding wedge, as you did on the shirt.

Draw in the bottom of the vest.

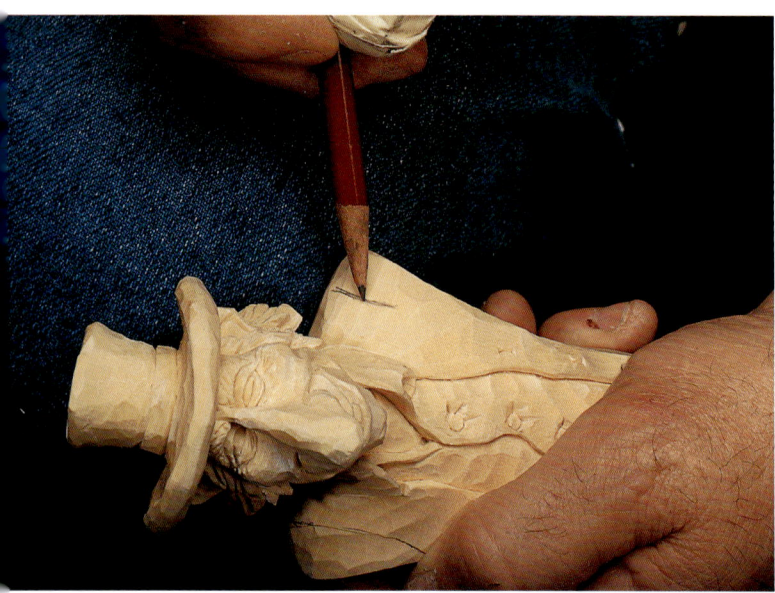

Draw in the armholes, front and back.

V-tool the pencil lines outlining the vest.

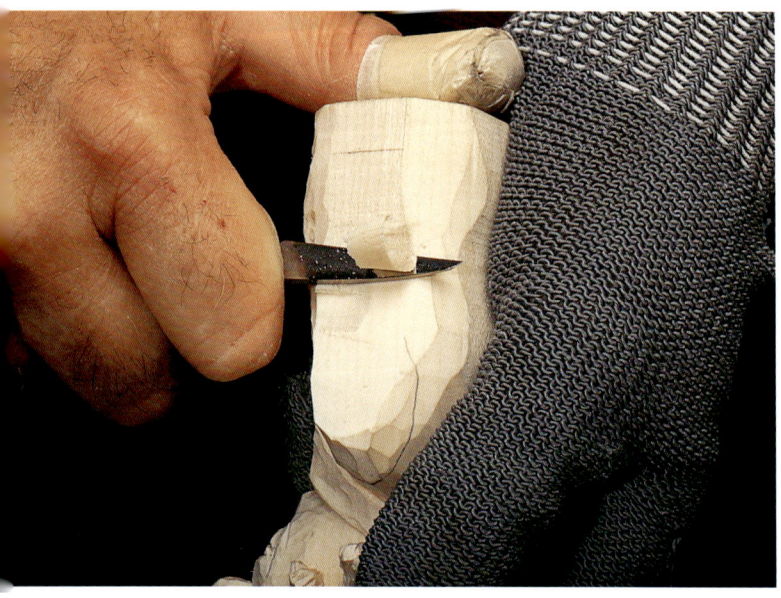

Clean up the rest of the body, taking away saw marks.

Lower the surface of the shirt so it appears to come from under the vest. Clean up the gouge marks with a knife.

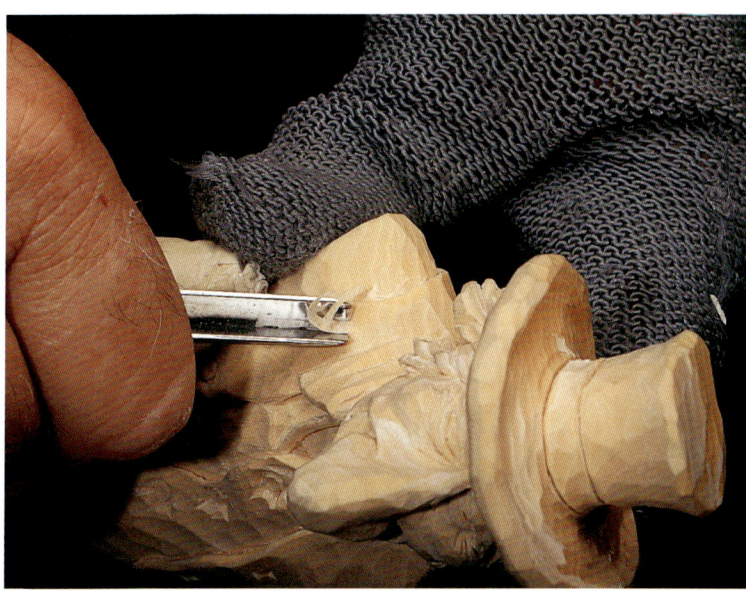

Undercut the vest sleeve openings and bottoms as you did before with a sliding wedge.

Finally add a few wrinkles to the vest using a v-tool. They tend to run randomly around the arm hole.

Ready for painting.

Painting

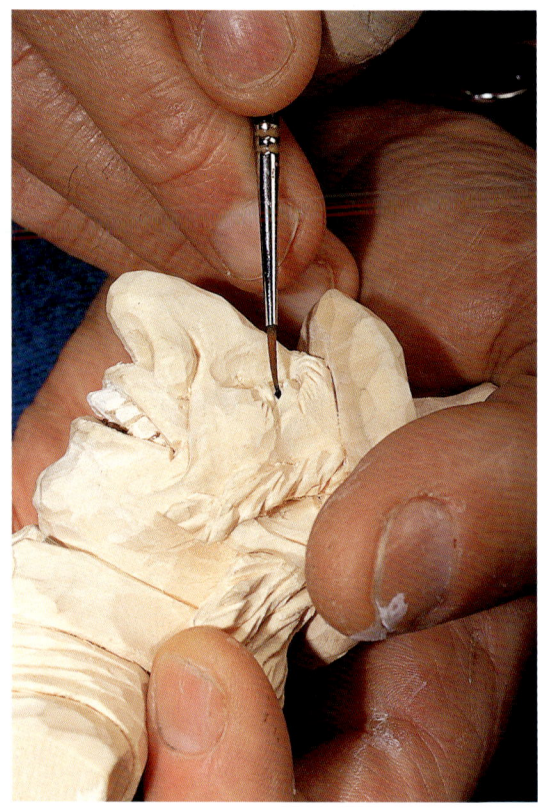

To begin the painting I apply the white. This includes the eyes, the teeth, and the tee-shirt on this carving. I use an acrylic wash that is slightly off white. Many carvers make the mistake of using a stark white on the eyes.

Next I do the pupil of the eye using full strength black acrylic paint. Because I've exaggerated the face to the left I will make him look to the left. Just a speck of black paint on the end of the brush makes the pupil.

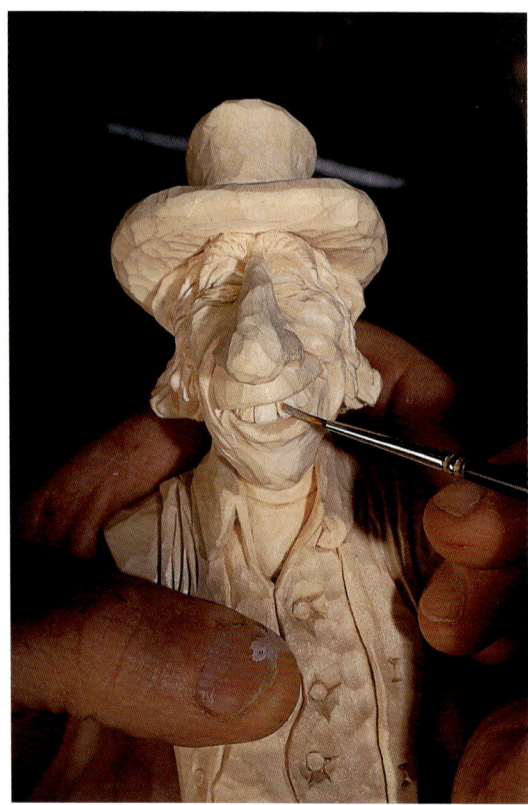

Continue with the teeth, remembering to paint underneath as well. Also do the t-shirt.

The result

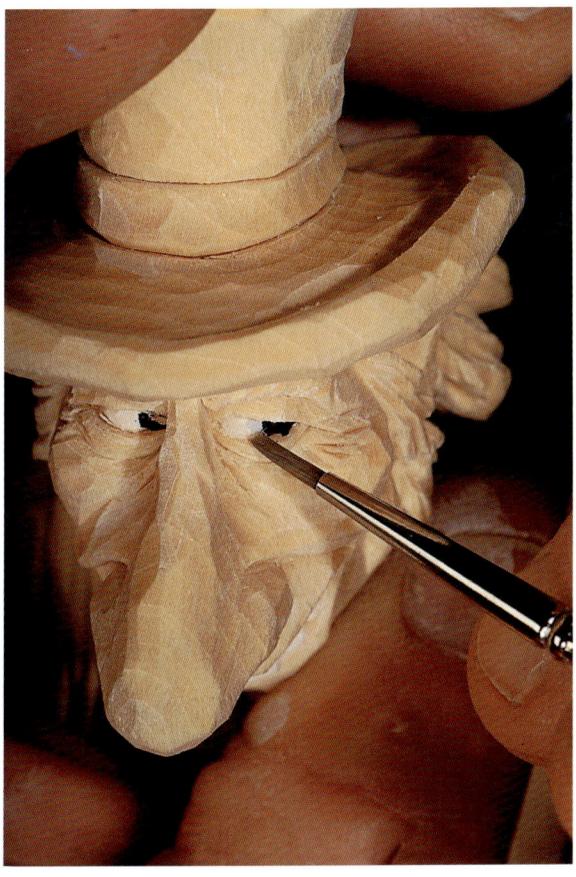

The iris is added with just a hint of paint on the brush. It goes onto the white around the pupil.

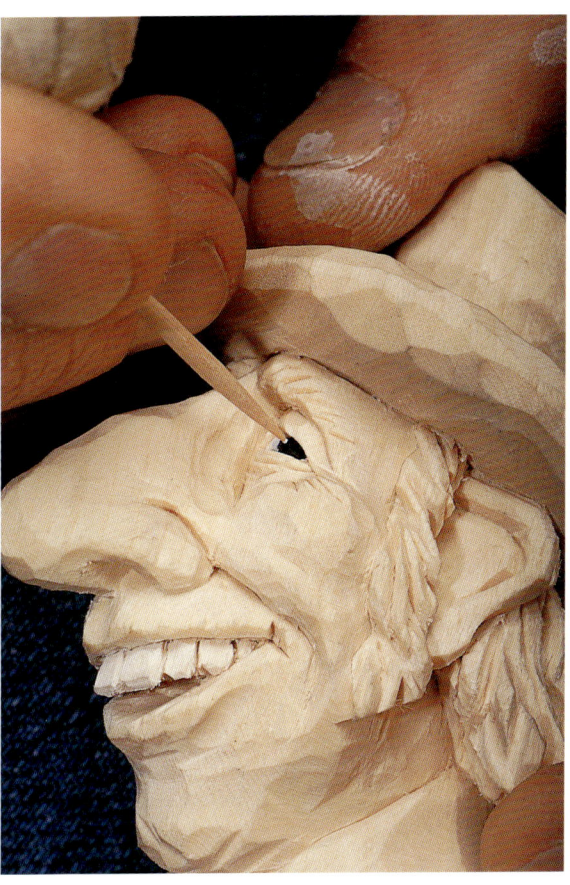

Apply a white dot of light with the point of a toothpick. Use full strength acrylic.

The result.

The result. The dot should be in the same relative position in each eye.

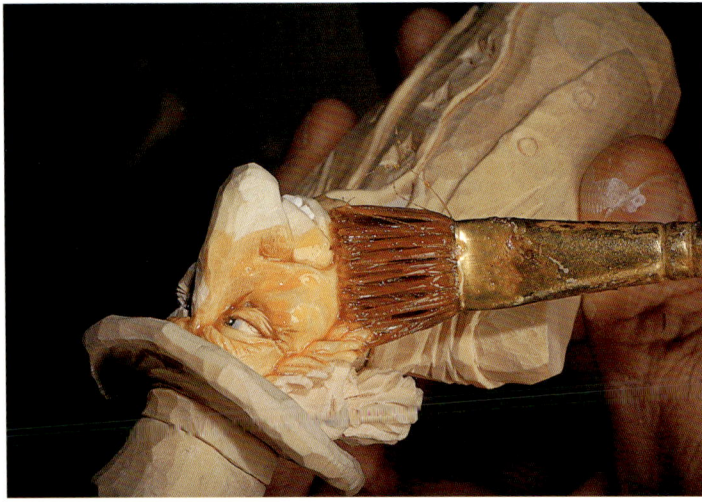

After the eyes have been painted I dip the carving in a mixture of linseed oil and raw sienna. It gives a base coat about the color of eastern pine. Usually I dip the carving in a vat of oil, but working in the studio I need to brush it on. Either way, cover the whole carving, including the eyes. You may have to work it into the hair. Remember, linseed oil in rags will cause spontaneous combustion in rags. Don't keep oily rags in your house.

Let the oil soak in for about five minutes and wipe off the excess. Be particularly careful not to leave any puddles.

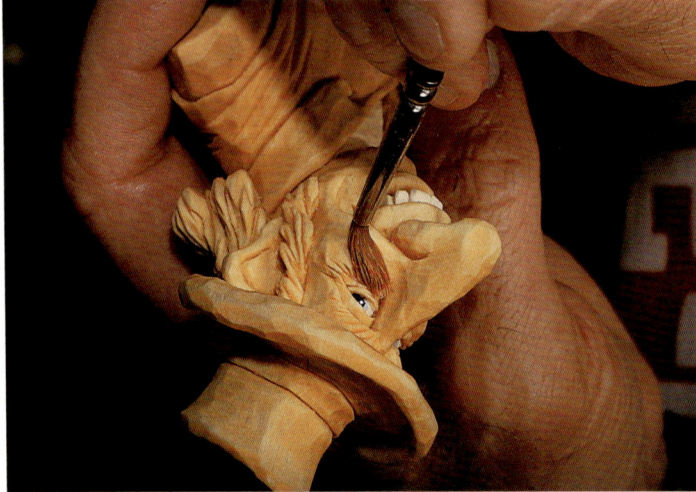

You can start painting right after you wipe it down. I start with the flesh areas using a medium flesh color with a touch of cadmium red added. All the acrylic paint from this point on is diluted to be a wash.

Next I add a little cad red to the cheeks, chin, the nose, the ears, eye sacks and anywhere else it looks a little pale. This gives a little life to the skin tones, but be careful not to create a clownish effect. Pick up just a hint of the red in the brush and apply it as a highlight.

The result.

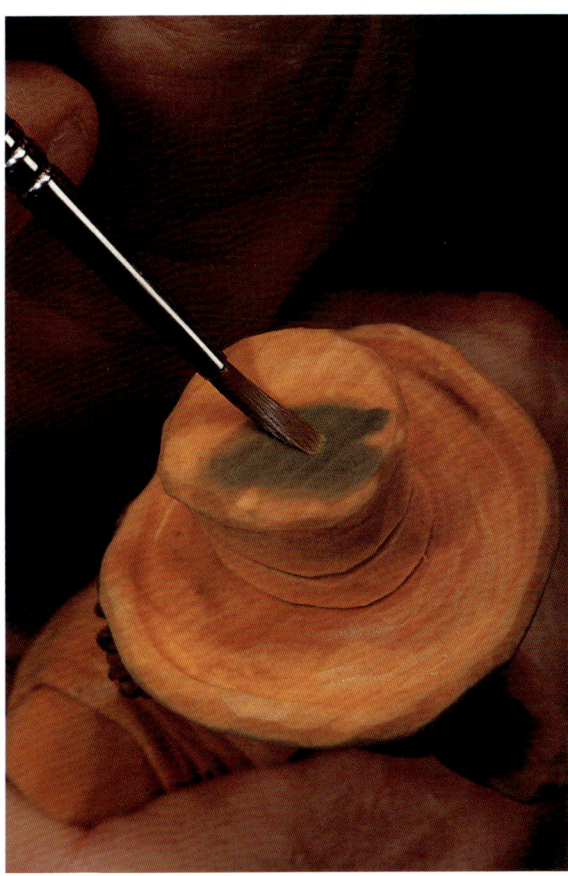

The hat is painted with a green wash, with the band left unpainted.

The hair is painted with a dark brown acrylic wash. Paint the sideburns, eyebrows, and hair.

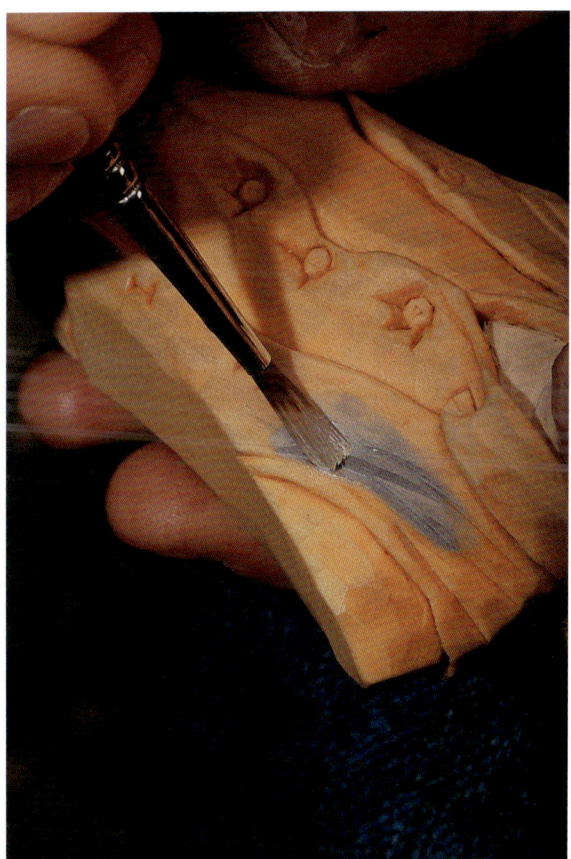

The vest is gray.

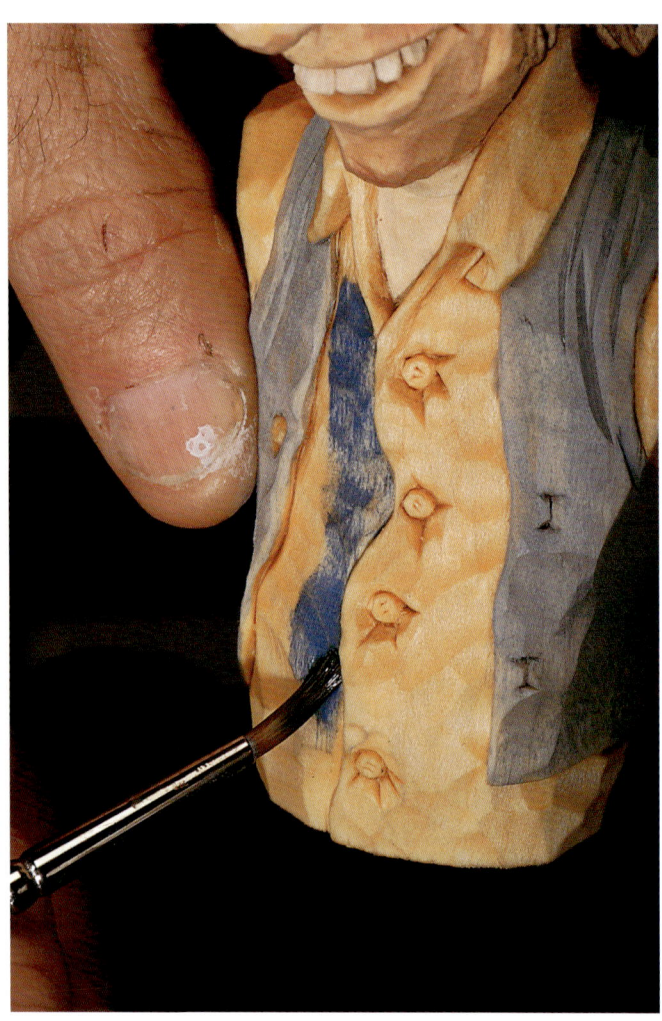

The shirt is blue.

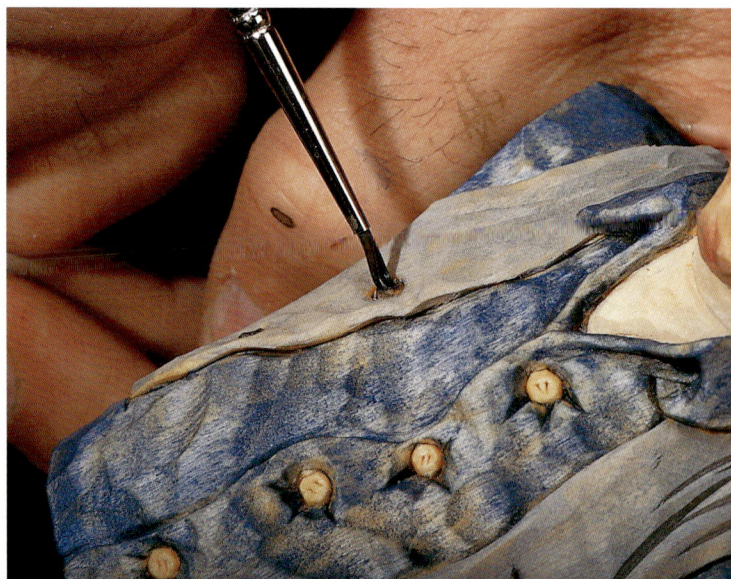

With a small amount of black on the brush, work the pigment into the buttons of the vest. I'm going to leave the shirt buttons natural.

The finished project

Gallery

Main project

Left,: boxer; right, clown.

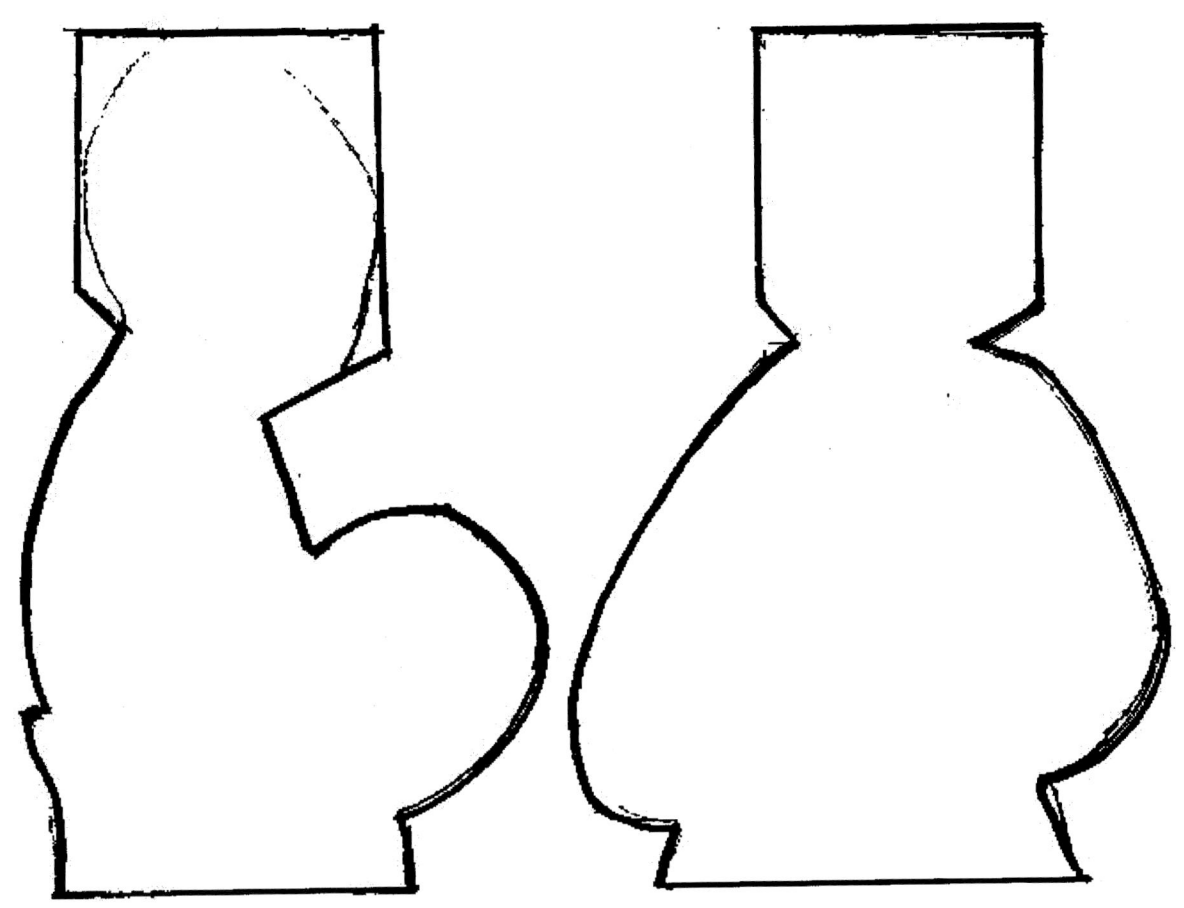

Boxer, 4-1/2" tall

Clown, 3-3/4" tall

Left, Ebo; center, Garrison; right: Garfield

Ebo, 5-3/4" tall

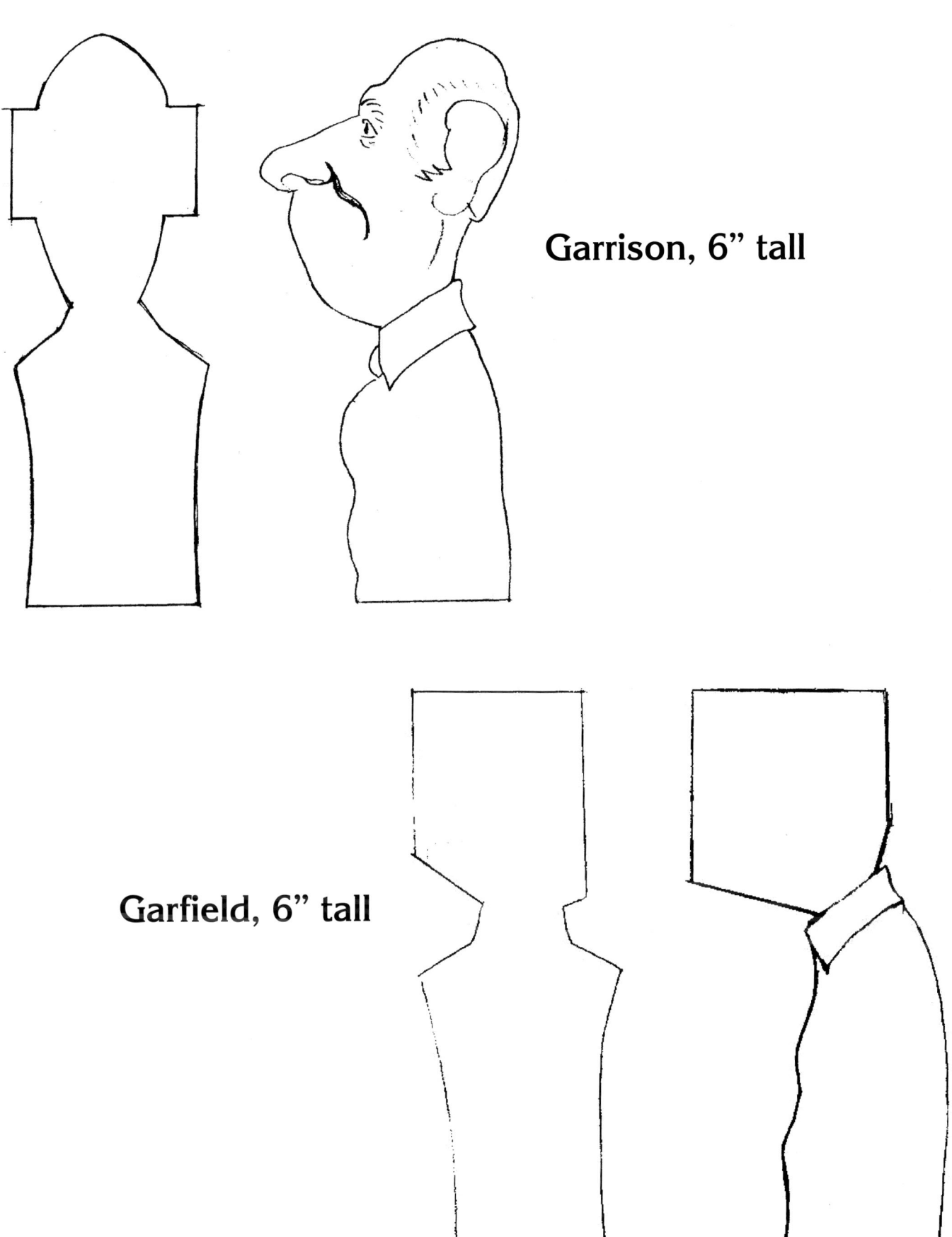

Garrison, 6" tall

Garfield, 6" tall

Left, Addisson; center, Cyril; right, Abbott.

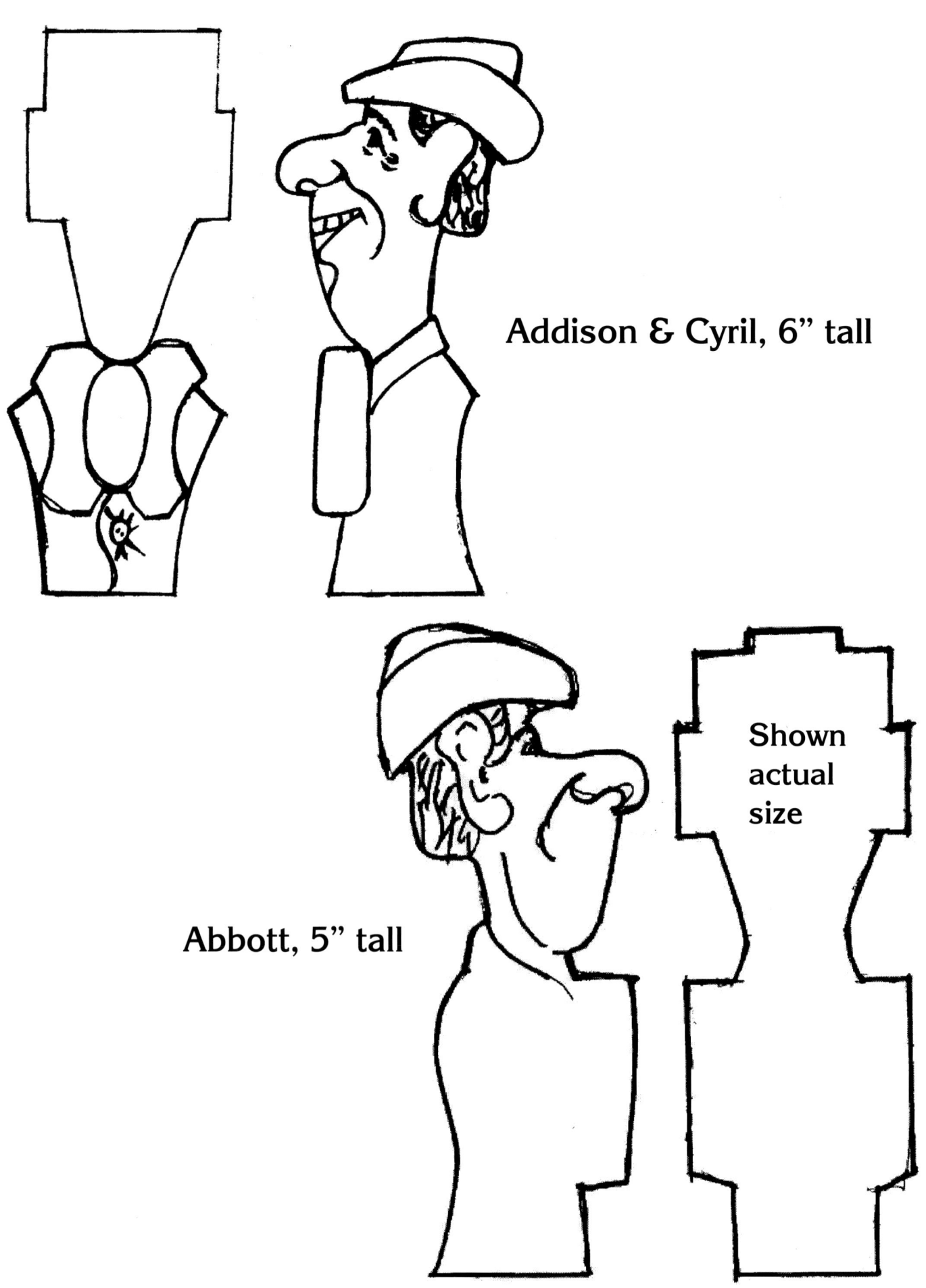

Addison & Cyril, 6" tall

Abbott, 5" tall

Shown
actual
size

Left: Anton; right, P.T. Bailey.

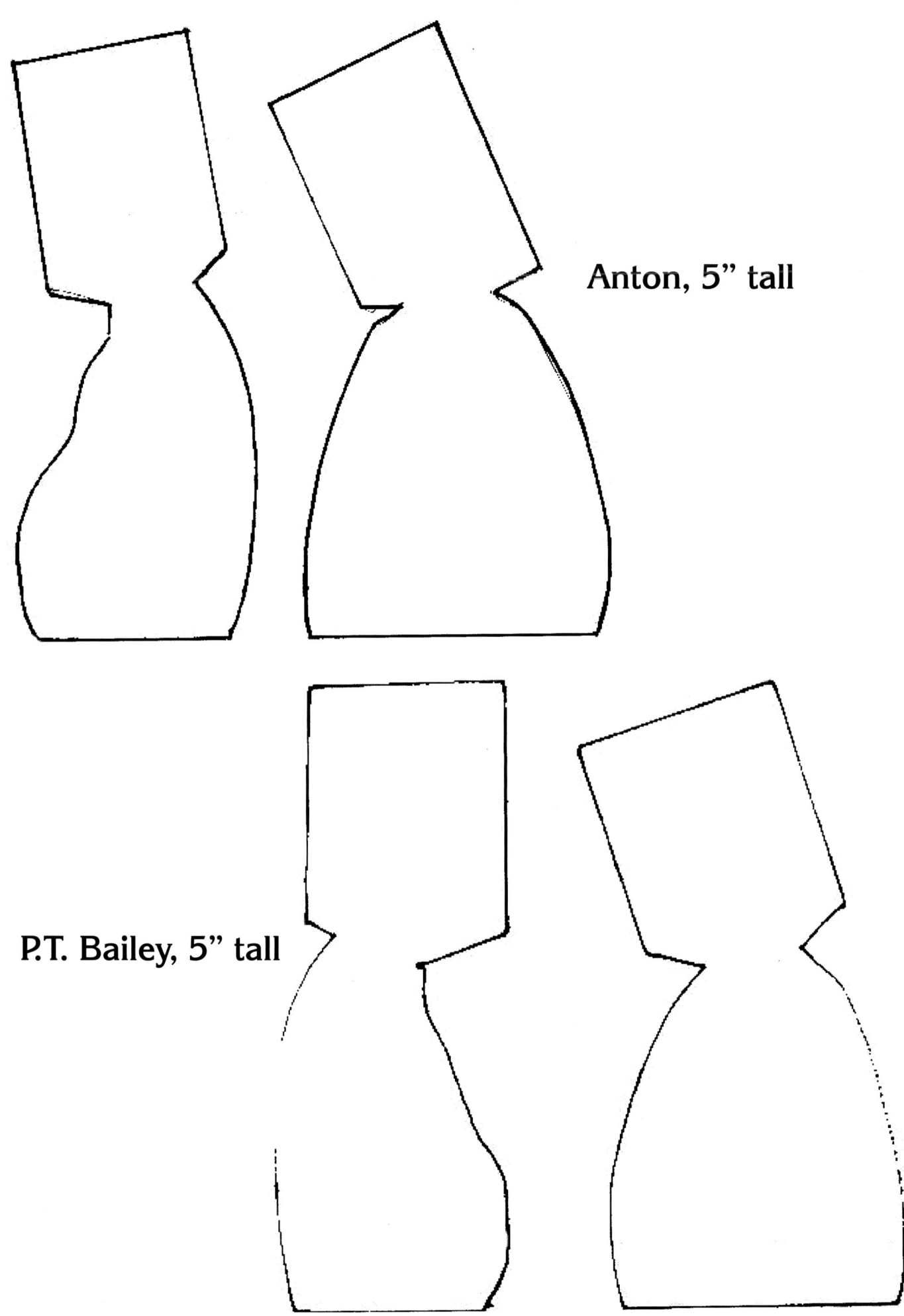

Anton, 5" tall

P.T. Bailey, 5" tall

Left: Slim; center, Cletus; right: Spense.

Cletus, 4-3/4" tall

Slim, 5-3/4" tall

Spense, 5-1/2" tall

Left to right: Peter, Rodney, Gaylord, Jake, and Hubbard

Peter, 4-1/4" tall

Rodney, 4-3/4" tall

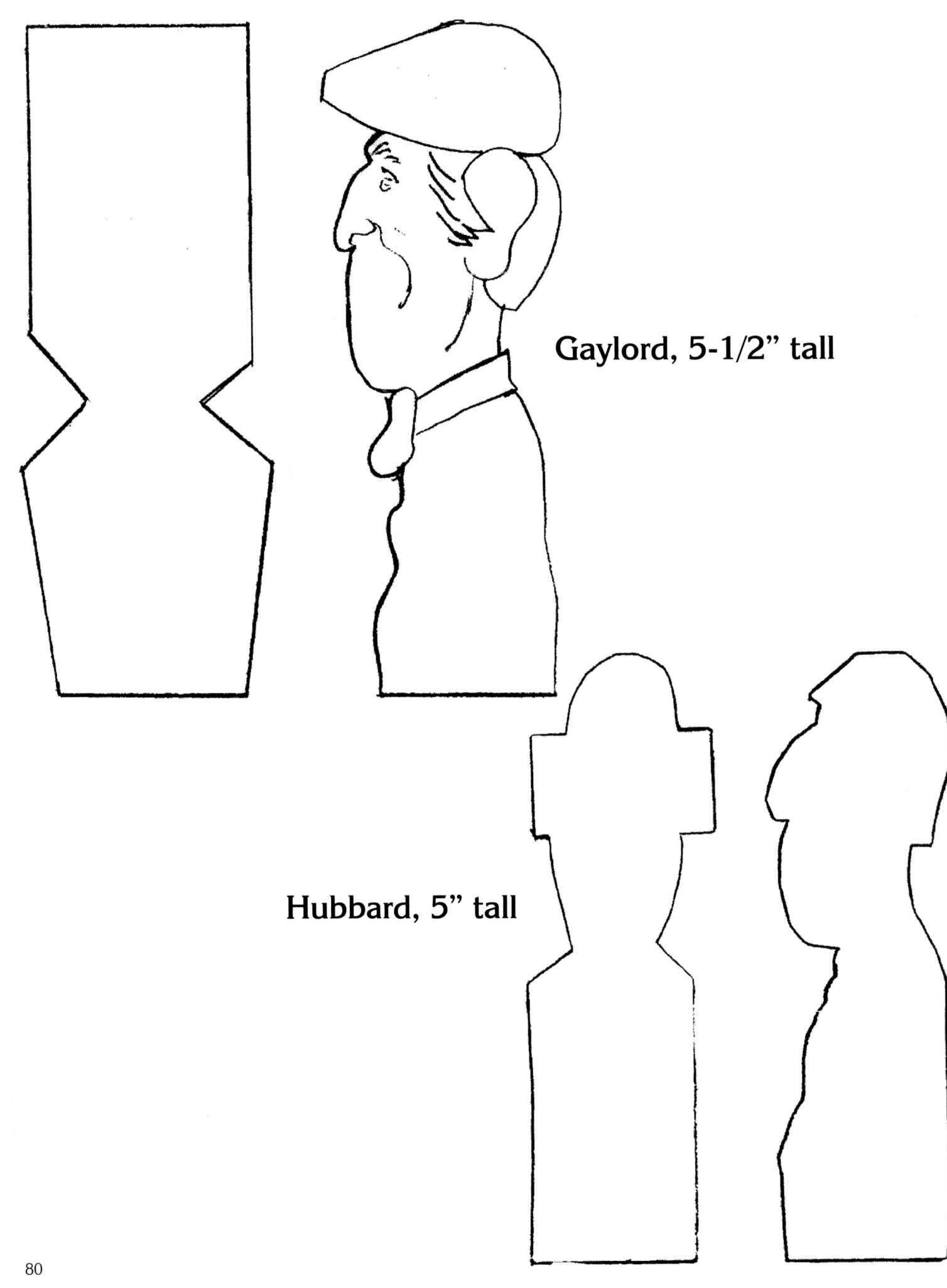

Gaylord, 5-1/2" tall

Hubbard, 5" tall